SAMUELS
ARISING

SAMUELS ARISING

WAKING UP TO GOD'S PROPHETIC CALL

KEITH COLLINS

SAMUELS ARISING: WAKING UP TO GOD'S PROPHETIC CALL

GENERATI◯NIMPACT
m i n i s t r i e s

PO Box 620084
Charlotte, NC 28262

For information or permissions contact:
Generation Impact Ministries
https://www.GenerationImpactMinistries.com

Cover design, editing, and layout by JJ Weller—JJWellerMedia.com

ISBN: **978-1-54397-877-3**

Second Edition: August 2019

10 9 8 7 6 5 4 3 2

CONTENTS

Foreword by Dr. Michael L. Brown (7)

Foreword by Evangelist Daniel Kolenda (11)

Chapter 1. A Samuel Generation (17)

Chapter 2. Samuels Asleep by the Altar (29)

Chapter 3. Samuels Awakening (55)

Chapter 4. The Spiritual DNA of the Samuel Generation (79)

Chapter 5. From Samuel to David (91)

Chapter 6. My Samuel Commitment (98)

Afterword: Walking Out Your Samuel Commitment (109)

About Keith Collins (116)

Acknowledgements (118)

Notes (120)

FOREWORD

BY DR. MICHAEL L. BROWN

Thirty years ago, when Leonard Ravenhill penned the foreword to my first revival-themed book, *The End of the American Gospel Enterprise*, he began with these words: "There is not much that has been written in recent years that has stirred me. This book stirred me. I read it with great profit. It is vibrant and has an anointing." That's exactly how I felt as I read this book. In fact, it not only stirred me. It convicted me to press into God afresh for a deeper personal encounter with the Lord. Oh, that all of us might burn passionately for Him!

I have known Keith Collins since 1997, first as a student in the *Brownsville Revival School of Ministry*, where he joined us with years of ministry experience already in his background, then as a member of our faculty and leadership team. Since then, he has served as pastor of our congregation and director of our ministry school, both appropriately named *FIRE*.

During these years of serving together, I have watched him mentor a generation of students and witnessed his pastoral heart in action in the church, so you can be sure that he is motivated by love as he speaks and writes. But it is that same love that burns within him as a prophetic voice and revivalist; a love that will not allow him to be silent when so many of God's people are asleep in the light. No! He must raise his voice like a trumpet and sound the alarm. As he says so clearly in this book (and as I have said in the past), "We need a rude awakening."

In the pages that follow, Keith will help you to identify areas of compromise and sleepiness in your own life—not to condemn you but to encourage and empower you to turn to the only one who can bring lasting change in your life. And he will set before you a glorious vision of just how the Lord Jesus can use you to make a radical impact on this generation. Isn't it time?

May you be among a multitude of Samuels who awaken today with a deep sense of prophetic destiny. This book will help show you the way.

Dr. Michael L. Brown, host of the Line of Fire radio broadcast and president of *FIRE School of Ministry Online*

FOREWORD
BY EVANGELIST DANIEL KOLENDA

I had a strange experience recently at a large conference our ministry hosted in Europe. When I arrived to preach, my driver took me to a back stadium entrance reserved for the speakers. Security was tight. A special badge was required to enter through that door, but my team assumed I wouldn't need one. After all, *we* were hosting the event. I was on the platform each night and easily seen on the large screens by all in attendance. "Your face is your badge," they told me. But the guard stationed at the door had a different opinion. He worked for the venue. He was not one of our team members. He didn't know me, and he was adamant—I could not enter without a badge. It was a comical sight. Inside the stadium, the people were waiting for me to preach. But I was stuck outside, unable to get into my own event!

In Revelation 3:20, Jesus said, "Behold, I stand at the door and knock" (ESV). As an evangelist, I've occasionally referenced these words in my evangelistic appeals. As powerful as this invitation is to the unsaved, it's important to remember that in the original context, Jesus was not speaking to the lost. He was speaking to His own people. Somehow, even in the earliest days—while the ink of the New Testament was still wet—Jesus was already outside the door of His own church knocking. It's a scene that would be comical if it weren't so sad. I believe this is the tragic picture Jesus wanted us to see. He is the host—the church is His—yet He is on the outside looking in. His words to them were unequivocal and severe. "I know your works: you are neither cold nor hot. Would that you were either cold or hot! So, because you are lukewarm, and neither hot nor cold, I will spit you out of my mouth. For you say, I am rich, I have prospered, and I need nothing, not realizing that you are wretched, pitiable, poor, blind, and naked" (Revelation 3:16-17 ESV).

It's a distinctive characteristic of human nature that we are ever like sheep—prone to stray. Many understand the words of *Come Thou Fount* by eighteenth-century poet Robert Robinson:

> *"Prone to wander, Lord, I feel it,*
> *Prone to leave the God I love..."*

It is exactly this propensity for backsliding that makes the prophet's voice so important for every generation. This is why God continues to raise voices who will speak prophetically to His people. Though separated by time, culture, language, and geography, the prophetic voices are remarkably similar.

In the Old Testament, Isaiah prophesies to Judah and Jerusalem: "Wash yourselves; make yourselves clean; remove the evil of your deeds from before my eyes" (Isaiah 1:16). The word of the Lord to Jeremiah was like a fire and a hammer that breaks rocks in pieces (see Jeremiah 23:29). Hosea implored his backslidden people to return to the Lord to be healed and revived (see Hosea 6:1). Ezekiel tells Israel to "repent and live" (Ezekiel 18:32 NASB). Similar exhortations are found from all the Old Testament prophets.

Opening the New Testament, we immediately encounter John the Baptist crying, "Repent, for the kingdom of heaven is at hand" (Matthew 3:2 ESV). Jesus takes up this theme in His own ministry, calling the people to repent and raising the bar for every prophet to come.

This tradition did not end with the close of Scripture—it has continued down through the centuries into modern times. Men like John Wesley, George Whitefield, and Charles Finney famously preached repentance with a fervor and passion that continues to provoke us today. And still, in our own generation, God has called men and women to communicate His heart to His people.

One of the many similarities between these prophetic voices is that in almost every instance, they were largely ignored or rejected by the people of their day. As Stephen asked before his martyrdom, "Which of the prophets did your fathers not persecute?" (Acts 7:52 ESV). It is very tempting to ignore the prophetic call to break up our fallow ground and return to the Lord. It is very easy to ignore Jesus knocking at the door of our hearts as He longs to come back into the center of His own church. That is why I appreciate the book you are reading so much. *Samuels Arising* is a back-to-the-basics reminder of what's important. I believe that in these pages, Keith Collins has stepped into the role of a prophet, calling God's people—you and me—back to our first love. As I read the powerful words on page after page, I felt a re-alignment happening in my own life. I could feel the passion coming through the text and stoking the fire in my own heart. What a precious gift!

When I was first filled with the Holy Spirit, one of the things I remember vividly is how much I loved those prophetic voices calling me to a closer walk with God. I loved His conviction. I loved His rebukes. They didn't discourage or frustrate me—they were a sign of His fatherly love. In Revelation 3:19, Jesus said to the church: "As many as I love, I rebuke and chasten" (KJV). Then He encouraged them to "be zealous and repent" (Revelation 3:19 KJV). Imagine that—being passionate about repentance! I believe one of the greatest signs of a healthy spiritual condition is that we are excited about pleasing

God. We want His correction, His conviction and His loving re-alignment in every area of our lives. Some of you will feel that way as you read this book. That's a good sign. Others will recoil—that is a very telling sign as well. Pay attention to how your heart reacts to the prophetic confrontation on the pages to follow. Allow it to be a sort of diagnostic test, and respond accordingly. Not only do I recommend this book—I suggest you read it again and again. Hear the urgent knocking at the door, and hear the Master's loving invitation to you. He who has an ear, let him hear what the Spirit says to the churches.

"Behold, I stand at the door and knock. If anyone hears my voice and opens the door, I will come in to him and eat with him, and he with me." (Revelation 3:20 ESV)

Evangelist Daniel Kolenda
President & CEO of *Christ for all Nations*

CHAPTER ONE

A Samuel Generation

Today's church *looks* better than ever on the outside. Our meetings are polished. Our media are masterful. Our sanctuaries are adorned with lights, smoke machines, and giant screens—but underneath the vain sheen of success, numbers, and accolades, millions of professing Christians are asleep. Like the Church of Sardis, we "have a name that [we] are alive" (Revelation 3:1 NASB)—we are drunk on the form of religion with its preachers, platforms, potlucks, and paychecks. But, the truth is that we "are dead" (Revelation 3:1 NASB)—the majority of churchgoers have yet to encounter God's transforming power. We need a rude awakening.

I believe God wants to awaken our generation to the reality of His glory once again—to interrupt our spiritual sleepiness, purify our sins, restore our gospel vision and catapult us into our original prophetic calling. That's the main focus of this book. But before we can experience such awakening, we must acknowledge our sleepy condition. Are you willing to look into the condition of the church—and yourself? I've traveled widely in churches, and I'll tell you what I've found. Many believers have sold out.

MINISTERS HAVE SOLD OUT TO A DILUTED GOSPEL

First, let's start with the ministry. Many ministers have sold out to a diluted gospel. Moved by ego, thousands of Christian leaders have bought into the gospel of ease, prosperity, fame, and fortune. Instead of preaching Jesus the Savior, they preach Jesus the Santa Claus. Seeking to cuddle their hearers, they say: "Come to Jesus! He will fix your problems, help your marriage, give you a better job, pay off your house, and heal your body." Forgetting the fear of God and the true gospel, they've created a false sense of security and a culture of compromise.

As a result, most modern churchgoers don't even know the basic facts of the gospel. For example, a 2018 study found that 52% of evangelicals believe "everyone sins a little, but most people are good by nature," while 51% believe "God accepts the worship of all religions, including Christianity, Judaism, and Islam."[1] Why don't one-half of evangelicals understand that all men are sinners and Jesus is the only Savior? Because they haven't been clearly taught. Ministers have sold out to a diluted gospel.

SELLING OUT TO THE CULTURE OF COMFORT

Other churches have sold out to the culture of comfort, becoming mere social clubs with Jesus as mascot. Wanting people to feel comfortable and loved, preachers have exchanged the fear of God for the entertainment of the world.

I remember one church meeting I attended. Before ministry time began, all the lights dimmed and huge screens lit up across the auditorium. What would they play on the screens—announcements, slides, sermon clips, or Christian music videos? No—visitors walked in to black and white footage of the Beatles singing *A Hard Day's Night*. No one seemed concerned, and some congregants even began to clap, sing, and scream like they were at a concert. But while they rejoiced, I grieved. All I could think was, "What in the world just happened?"

I witnessed an alarming truth that day: the modern church has assimilated to the world. Many ministers believe they must use the world's culture—its expressions, music, fashion, and folly—to draw the world in. They aim for comfort but avoid conviction. They make sinners feel all is well; that they never have to *truly* decide for Christ. They will compromise almost anything to "reach the world"—and therein, they show that *they themselves still must be reached*. They've forgotten the true knowledge of God. But it gets even worse.

SELLING OUT TO SIN

Others have sold out to sin. Sure, many preachers *permit evil*—they neglect to preach about sin, hell, eternal separation from God, the cross, repentance, and very obvious commands of God. But even more frighteningly, many professed ministers now *promote evil*.

One such case especially grieves me. A prominent worship band seems to have tremendous anointing. Thousands gather to hear their music, encounter God, and receive spiritual refreshing. During the concerts, the musicians appear enveloped in God's presence as they pour out their hearts in passionate songs about surrender, God's love, and more. But after the large crowds leave, while still in the glow of the exciting meeting, the band members drive off to bars to get drunk. They do this with no conviction or regret—feeling great and boasting of their "freedom in Christ."

Adding to this, thousands of gay "pastors" have flooded America's religious world as entire denominations have embraced the homosexual agenda. 1 in 7 pastors and 1 in 5 youth pastors admit to currently using pornography.[2] I've heard many ministers mock Christian leaders of prior centuries, calling them "antiquated" and "legalistic" for their dedication to the gospel, prayer, and holiness. An exaggerated grace message has desensitized pulpit and pew alike to the Holy Spirit's conviction. There's no question—today's ministers need a prophetic awakening. But it's not only the ministry.

SLEEPY PREACHERS; SLEEPY PARISHIONERS

I firmly believe an adage: "So goes the ministry, so goes the people." Compromised ministers breed compromised churches. If Christian leaders fail to clearly preach the biblical gospel, the church will tolerate and even promote sin. Just that has happened in today's Christian world.

Jesus promised that His people would be "the light of the world" (Matthew 5:14 NIV). In other words, God's true people would live differently than those around them. God has not called us to fit in but to stand out! Our purpose is to shine a light of eternal reality in the midst of a perishing world. Tragically, many professing Christians are no different than the lost.

Leonard Ravenhill said, "To be spiritually minded is joy and peace. Yet to be statistically minded in addition can be very disturbing."[3] Statistics reveal just how much professing Christians live like the world. Jesus clearly forbids flippant divorce (Matthew 5:31-33), but 32% of professing "born-again Christians" have divorced at least once—almost as much as non-believing adults.[4] Jesus warns against the lust of the eyes (Matthew 5:28), yet 64% of Christian men and 15% of Christian women claim they watch pornography at least once a month.[5] Shockingly, only 1 in 3 professing Christians who use porn feel any guilt for their digital decadence, and only 19% claim they are "currently trying to stop."[6]

As ministers have permitted sin, professing Christians have pursued sin. Recently, a friend e-mailed me with a striking example. He wrote:

> We've supported a church in [a South American country] for many years. We ministered there recently, and a church member invited us to her home to pray over her 'family'. When we entered the home, we saw a man sitting in the kitchen. She introduced him as her "pareja"—her unmarried romantic partner. It turns out she had lived with this man (an unbeliever) for many years, and had two children with him. She expressed that she finally wanted to marry, but her partner was not so willing.

> Our hearts sank to realize this woman had been allowed to live such a tragic lifestyle while actively involved in the church. We felt even more shocked when we spoke to the pastor. He told us that most of congregation's women (even those involved in ministry) were in the same heartbreaking situation. We've known many of those women for years, and now we've discovered they were in fornication or adultery all along. Many of the church's children were conceived this way. I've learned to preach clearly about cohabitation, fornication, and adultery because these issues are rampant—even in respectable denominations.

These are monumental problems. Without a prophetic awakening, gross sin will continue to grow in our midst.

A PROPHET AWAKENED; A NATION RESTORED

In Samuel's day, Israel's spiritual climate had also ebbed cold. Idolatry crept in among the people, and sinful compromise flooded the ministry. Eli the high priest welcomed wickedness in the temple: his sons Hophni and Phinehas perverted the sacrificial offering system and committed sexual immorality in God's temple presence, yet Eli refused to restrain them (see 1 Samuel 3:13). As a result of spiritual compromise, "the word of the Lord was rare in those days; there was no frequent vision" (1 Samuel 3:1 ESV).

Eli's compromise had spread far and wide, as we see in the life of young Samuel. God chose Samuel to the priesthood and set him under Eli's care in the temple. Yet "Samuel did not yet know the Lord" (1 Samuel 3:7 NASB). A fog rested upon the priesthood; Eli's spiritual leniency had created a lukewarm, watered down environment devoid of spiritual fire. As a result, Samuel's soul remained dim. He lived in the presence of the ark of the covenant, he learned under the tutelage of the high priest, yet he still didn't know God, and the word of the Lord was dead to him. Just like many reading this book, Samuel was frozen in the midst of fire.

Yet soon God *spoke* to Samuel, breaking an age of prophetic silence. In the middle of the night while he lay by the ark of God, a voice called "Samuel!" The young man did not recognize the voice, but elderly Eli did. Though backslidden, Eli still had enough memory and spiritual sensitivity to recognize that God had called Samuel. So Eli instructed the young man, "Go, lie down, and if he calls you, you shall say, 'Speak, Lord, for your servant hears' " (1 Samuel 3:9 ESV).

Neither Eli nor Samuel expected the fierce word God intended to speak. God would "do a thing in Israel at which the two ears of everyone who [heard it would] tingle . . . to punish [Eli's] house forever, for the iniquity that he knew, because his sons were blaspheming God, and he did not restrain them" (1 Samuel 3:11, 13 ESV). Samuel's first prophetic assignment was to collide with the dead religious order of his generation; to stand before his compromised spiritual father and say, "Judgment is coming, and there's no sacrifice or offering you can give to turn the tide. You've gone too far."

Soon, God would speak through Samuel "to all Israel" (1 Samuel 4:1 ESV), birthing Israels' great prophetic movement and restoring God's purposes in His people. Awakened by God out of sleep, Samuel would now wake Israel out of sleep, opening a new dimension of heavenly revelation and spiritual vitality. As a result of this revelation, Israel would begin to reflect Yahweh once again.

A SAMUEL GENERATION ARISING

Every generation has its sleepers—even in the church. In the face of compromise, many believers have lost hope. They believe the tide could never turn; that we'll never see another genuine, shattering move of God in our land. But you need not despair. In the midst of spiritual sleepiness, God remains faithful to His own glory. God will raise up an army of voices like Samuel to sound an alarm to the sleeping church; in this way, God will preserve for Himself "a remnant chosen by grace" (Romans 11:5 NIV).

Yes, just as young Samuel woke up to God's voice, I believe a whole Samuel generation is waking up—and they will awaken the multitudes to the reality of God. As Samuel received a revelation of God, these Christians will receive a revelation of Jesus' glory and walk in true spiritual authority marked by deep passion for Him. As Samuel despised religious falsehood, they will despise man-made religion and the death it breeds, and yearn fiercely for intimacy with God Himself. As Samuel devoted his life to obedience, they will love true holiness, purity, and righteousness and carry the cross as a lifestyle, not merely a one-time experience.

Once awakened, they will awaken others; they will carry an unusual boldness, anointing, and authority by which they will accomplish the works of Jesus in their generation. As Samuel, these Christians will totally depend on God and utterly resist ambition, independence, and idolatry. And as Samuel, they will carry God's heart; the prophetic burden will burn within. They will not sit on this burden but will live as God's apostolic messengers. They've encountered the All-Consuming Fire and received from Him the call to *go* and do the works of

Jesus. They will not sell out to anyone; no, it will be said of them: "They overcame him by the blood of the Lamb, and by the word of their testimony; and they loved not their lives unto the death" (Revelation 12:11 KJV).

God used Samuel to awaken his generation, and I believe God wants to use *you* to awaken the world from its slumber. Let's study God's Word to learn how to become a Samuel generation.

CHAPTER TWO

Samuels Asleep by the Altar

The lamp of God had not yet gone out, and Samuel was lying down in the temple of the Lord where the ark of God was.
(1 Samuel 3:3 NASB)

From Moses until Eli, God's holy presence dwelled especially in one place—by the ark of God in the tabernacle. In past generations, God had allowed His weighty glory to rest there, causing holy fear in all who drew near.

But times had changed. Eli the high priest had tolerated sin, allowing his sons to have sex before God's temple presence. Eli thus exchanged God's holy presence for mere form and ritual. God's glory waned in the temple. Whereas men of old once trembled in fear before God's altar, now young Samuel could peacefully sleep by it. He was in the right setting, had the right doctrine, and had a true calling—but he "did not yet know the Lord" (1 Samuel 3:7 ESV).

Thousands of professing Christians are asleep by the altar today too. I don't mean that they lack pure doctrine, ministry anointing, clever messages, or exciting meetings. You can experience all of those things without ever meeting the Lord Himself. The question is not if you live near the altar; instead, do you know the God of the altar? Maybe you know about Him. Maybe you even live around Him. But *do you know Him?* As evangelist Steve Hill said, "Religion is hanging around the cross. Christianity is getting on the cross."[7]

To realize our true condition, we must abandon a superficial, surface-level approach to Christianity. Many feel spiritual because they go to church, read the Bible, or live generally moral lives. But spiritual sleep occurs much deeper within the passions of the heart.

Spiritual sleepiness is a state wherein one has knowledge about God but lacks God Himself; wherein one has the outward display of religion but no inward burning passion for Christ. Spiritual sleepyheads are marked by their *dullness*— they live in close proximity to God but have no sensitivity to God's heart. For this reason, Jesus said of spiritual sleepers: "These people honor me with their lips, but their hearts are far from me" (Matthew 15:8 NIV).

In the First and Second Great Awakenings, most professing Christians were spiritually asleep. They had attended church from birth, knew the Bible and Bible doctrine, and lived generally upright lives, but they didn't know God. Then,

God began to awaken prophetic voices akin to Samuel—men like Charles G. Finney, George Whitefield, John Wesley, and Jonathan Edwards. God used these firebrands to awaken their generations to the transforming gospel of Jesus Christ.

Today's professing Christians don't differ much from the sleepers of past generations. Many churchgoers have simply embraced Grandma's religion. Thus, they've slept all their lives. Others were once awakened but have since "left [their] first love" (Revelation 2:4 NASB). These too are spiritually asleep. The question is—where are you? Are you spiritually asleep? I want to share with you some clear symptoms of spiritual sleep so that you can know your spiritual state *without a doubt. As you read this chapter, be honest with yourself, or this book will be of no benefit to you.* I charge you with the words of revivalist Charles G. Finney:

And now . . . will you break up your fallow ground? . . . If you do not do this, and get prepared, you can go no further with me in this course of lectures . . . you must make thorough work upon this point, or all I have further to say will do you little good. Nay, it will only harden and make you worse. If [you continue] with unbroken hearts, you need not expect to be benefited by what I shall say . . . If you do not do this, I charge you with having forsaken Christ, with refusing to repent and do your first work.[8]

Reader, I plead with you: be bold, open your heart to God's conviction, and if you find you're spiritually asleep, get ready to return to your first love. If you turn from spiritual sleepiness, God will awaken you to His glory, purify you from sin, arrest your heart with the true gospel, and ignite His calling within you. You will be a Samuel in your generation.

SYMPTOM #1: FASCINATION WITH ENTERTAINMENT

The first symptom of spiritual sleepiness is a fascination with entertainment. The battle of the ages is for the passions of humanity. If you show me how you prioritize your time, I'll show you what you're passionate about. In fact, what you devote most of your free time to, you *worship*.

How does this play out in our lives? An awakened Christian is primarily fascinated with the holiness and beauty of Jesus. Jesus has supremacy in their heart and life. Over-whelmed by Christ, they have no need to seek other places for joy. But sleepy Christians lack the joy of intimacy with God, so they seek fulfillment in fleshly appetites and entertainment. Some professing Christians spend most of their free time watching television or browsing social networks. Many of those same people almost never take extended time to meet with God in prayer. Leonard Ravenhill's common statement explains their issue well: "Entertainment is the devil's substitute for joy."

Tragically, the modern church system lives drunk on worldliness. Professing Christians *must* be entertained. They need the right lights, smoke machines, sound, and music to enjoy a spiritual gathering. Few notice this trend until they leave its vain glow. For instance, many African and Indian Christians don't have such 'exquisite' taste in church meetings. I've preached in those countries (and others) under trees in blazing heat. God's glory often fell much stronger in those settings than in America's high-tech sanctuaries.

Our high-tech meetings often give professing Christians a false sense of euphoria, causing the spiritual snores to grow louder. When a sleepy Christian visits such a gathering, the lasers, smoke and pounding music give them a sense of release. They get their false religious fix and feel everything is okay. But it's all smoke and mirrors (pun intended). As soon as a trial hits their life, their spiritual sleepiness comes to light. They quickly fall away because they never had true intimacy with God—only a hyped experience.

Consequences of Fascination with Entertainment

Various consequences follow a fascination with entertainment. First, you lose your ability to see Jesus as He is. He becomes a spiritual mascot instead of the glorious King, Savior, Lord, and God. As a result, you fall out of fellowship with Him. You may go to church, preach, or even write Christian books—but if you invest your passions in this world, you will fall out of touch with the Lord.

Another consequence is that you enter into the dangerous cycle of compromise. When you let the world in, it changes you. You begin to condone things that would have repulsed you in a time of spiritual revival. You try to justify them; you "suppress the truth in unrighteousness" (Romans 1:18 NASB) because you know otherwise your common sense will condemn you. If you continue in this long enough, you inevitably pull others into your error.

Test Yourself for Symptom #1

Where do you stand? Are you fascinated with entertainment? Your priorities reveal your passions—so, how do you spend your leisure time? Do you spend most of your free time honoring Jesus, or entertaining yourself?

What type of entertainment do you consume? It's not wrong to enjoy clean entertainment within healthy, temperate boundaries—but some forms of entertainment will hinder your pursuit of God. Do you consume media that run counter to biblical teaching? Are you entertained by things that are *rebellious against Christ and the Bible?* Are you feasting on books, music, shows, movies, and art that promote fornication, adultery, theft, lies, and more? That shows where you are. If you're fascinated by entertainment, you're likely spiritually asleep.

My Spiritual Diagnosis:

_____

_____

_____

_____

_____

_____

_____

SYMPTOM #2: A SELFISH, INWARD LIFE-FOCUS

The second symptom of spiritual sleepiness is a selfish, inward life-focus. We have a selfish life-focus if we come to God for our own good, blessing, happiness, and prosperity instead of His glory.

Many churchgoers have no true heart for God Himself. He is the means to their selfish ends, not their ultimate goal. They come to church, read the Bible, and pray—but not to please God. They perform these spiritual exercises believing they will lead to their own success, promotion, and blessing. In fact, their entire relationship with God is conditional. They will follow God if He blesses and prospers them, but they will run as soon as God providentially removes His hand of blessing.

Many such people are victims of a diluted gospel. Much preaching today is all about the Unholy Trinity—"me, myself, and I." Preachers declare: "If you come to Jesus, He'll heal your body, make you happy, and make you a better you." God does all of those things—but that is not the gospel. You can't focus on self and Jesus at the same time.

The gospel is a message about Jesus: "Christ died for our sins according to the Scriptures . . . he was buried, [and] was raised on the third day according to the Scriptures" (1 Corinthians 15:3-4 NIV). However, few realize that Jesus died to save us from our selfish approach to life: "[Jesus] died for all, that those who live should no longer live for themselves but for him who died for them and was raised again" (2 Corinthians 5:15 NIV). In other words, the true gospel requires radical surrender. To live, you must die. We only find true life and fulfillment if we die to self, surrender to Christ, and rest in His finished work on the cross which doesn't change according to our feelings.

Consequences of a Selfish Life-Focus

Self-focused churchgoers miss out on *the burden of the Lord*. It's extremely difficult to hear God's heart for *others* when you ascribe to a gospel that's all about *you*. When you constantly dream of *your own* comfort, peace, blessing, fulfillment, and prosperity, what room do you have for God's burden for the lost? If you fall under the spell of self-focus, it will be impossible for God to give you His heart for lost souls. That is a tragedy of all tragedies.

Test Yourself for Symptom #2

How about you? Do you have a selfish, inward life-focus? Do you believe a self-centered gospel? Are you serving God based on what He can do for you, or based on who He is? Are you serving God because you need a blessing, a job, a miracle, more money, or happiness? If so, you're very likely spiritually asleep. It's time to wake up.

My Spiritual Diagnosis:

_____

_____

_____

_____

_____

_____

SYMPTOM #3: NEGLECT OF PRAYER

The third symptom of spiritual sleepiness is neglect of prayer. Awakened Christians fiercely desire the presence of God. They find no greater joy than to worship and adore Him. They have no greater longing than to experience His glory, holiness, love, and power. They don't merely want spiritual peripherals; they can't bear to worship God at a distance. They must dwell right in the midst of the All-Consuming Fire, for they feel their home lies beyond the veil, in the holy of holies.

Sleepy Christians know very little of this burning passion for prayer. They may pray at times, but usually only to make petitions. All their prayers sum up to one word: "Gimme!" The greatest reason for this lack of true prayer is sin. As John Bunyan said, "Prayer will make a man cease from sin, or sin will entice a man to cease from prayer."[9] You can't watch women take their clothes off and have a deep prayer life. It just doesn't work.

Consequences of Neglecting Prayer

Many negative consequences spring from neglect of prayer. First, if you neglect prayer, you will open the door to backsliding. You might not commit adultery, watch pornography, use drugs, or get drunk—but you'll certainly backslide in heart. You will cease loving Jesus supremely, and lesser lovers will take charge of your passions. You will begin to prostitute yourself with other gods—the gods of entertainment, ego, sex, pride, position, and more.

Second, if you stop praying, you'll soon stop hearing God's voice. A prayerless church is a powerless church, and ceases to be a prophetic church. If we lose prayer, we lose our prophetic edge. If we lose our prophetic edge, we become nothing more than a hollow religious form.

Relationships require quality time. I spend quality time with my wife to maintain our passion and connection. Many couples go through the motions, live in the same house, pay bills, and have children together, but have no passion for each other. Why? Because they don't prioritize quality time. The same applies to our relationship with God. To grow in intimacy with God, we must prioritize quality time with Him. If not, our relationship will grow cold.

Test Yourself for Symptom #3

How is your prayer life? Do you prioritize prayer? Do you have a discipline of prayer? What is the quality of your prayer life? Do you mainly offer petitions, or do you actually spend quality time in His presence, adoring, worshiping, and listening to Him? These questions should clearly reveal your true spiritual condition. If you neglect prayer, you're likely spiritually asleep.

My Spiritual Diagnosis:

_____

_____

_____

_____

_____

_____

_____

SYMPTOM #4: A LACK OF BURDEN FOR SOULS

The fourth symptom of spiritual sleepiness is *a lack of burden for lost souls*. Many Christians have sympathy for the perishing masses. They look at the world, see its lostness, feel sorry for souls who will go to hell, and generally desire their salvation. But awakened Christians have more than mere human sympathy: they carry the fiery burden of the Lord's heart. Yes, when God awakens you, He soon causes you to feel His heart for a dying world. You become *truly* prophetic by nature; consumed and possessed with *His* great longing for the salvation of lost souls. Feeling what God feels, you receive a deep and innate passion for God's mission.

All great prophets of scripture and missionaries of history have experienced this awesome burden for souls. Jeremiah experienced it, and cried out—"My anguish, my anguish! I writhe in pain!" (Jeremiah 4:19 ESV). C.T. Studd experienced it, and cried out: "I want to run a rescue shop within a yard of hell!"[10] These men felt so overwhelmed with God's burden that they had no choice but respond. Eaten up by God's very passion, they *had to* reach out and preach the gospel to the lost. World evangelism wasn't merely a noble idea—it became a vital part of their very identity. Missionary evangelist Oswald J. Smith put it this way in his book *The Revival We Need*:

> Can we travail for a drowning child, but not for a perishing soul? It is not hard to weep when we realize that our little one is sinking below the surface for the last time. Anguish is spontaneous then. Nor is it hard to agonize when we see the casket containing all that we love on earth borne out of the home. Ah, no; tears are natural at such a time. But oh, to realize and know that souls, precious, never dying souls, are perishing all around

us, going out into the blackness of darkness and despair, eternally lost, and yet to feel no anguish, shed no tears, know no travail! How cold are our hearts! How little we know of the compassion of Jesus![11]

Keith Green often said, "This generation of Christians is responsible for this generation of souls on earth." Hell enlarges itself daily, and the church is partly at fault. Never-dying souls are flooding into hell—can you bear to keep the gospel silent? Can you bear to go on living for yourself—to remain stoic, dead, and religious—while a dying world plunges into the flames?

Test Yourself for Symptom #4

Do you lack a burden for the lost? When was the last time you shed a tear for a dying soul? Have you received the burden of the Lord? Do you feel mere human sympathy for the perishing—or do you feel God's very sorrow for them? Furthermore, when was the last time you shared the gospel with an unbeliever? Have you ever shared the gospel with *anyone*? If you lack God's burden for souls, you are likely spiritually asleep.

My Spiritual Diagnosis:

_____

_____

_____

_____

_____

_____

SYMPTOM #5: COMPROMISE

The fifth symptom of spiritual sleepiness is compromise. Compromise is disobedience to your conscience.

Compromises of Commission

Many people condone or practice things that secretly violate conscience. This is called a *compromise of commission*. Speaking of this, Paul said: "Whatever is not from faith is sin" (Romans 14:23 NASB). John Wesley explained it this way: "Whatever a man does without a full persuasion of its lawfulness, it is sin to him."[12]

Modern churchgoers compromise in many ways. Many boldly dive into the traps of the world despite their knowledge of God's Word. Some compromise with their eyes through lust or ungodly forms of entertainment; others with their bodies through sexual perversion; others with their money, words, time, and more. This is a *sure symptom* of spiritual sleep.

Few sincere Christians compromise in this way quickly. Instead, the change is slow and subtle. First, they leave their first love by neglecting intimacy with God. Then, they start to make decisions based on fleshly desires instead of spiritual ones. Soon, fleshly desires override their spiritual appetites altogether. "When lust has conceived, it gives birth to sin; and when sin is accomplished, it brings forth death" (James 1:15 NASB). They become double-minded—Jesus remains a part of their life, but no longer sits on the throne of their passions.

They begin to enjoy practices and ideas that once grieved them. Soon, they justify themselves by falsely interpreting the Word of God. Many hide their sins by declaring "liberty in Christ" to do what they want.

Compromises of Omission

Many who will not compromise by *commission* still compromise by *omission*. James said, "To one who knows the right thing to do and does not do it, to him it is sin" (James 4:17 NASB). In other words, once you know God's call, spiritual laziness is compromise. This proves much more common today. Few churchgoers will openly practice gross sins—but *many* professing Christians neglect prayer, Bible study, worship to God, evangelism, fellowship, and works of service.

Consequences of Compromise

The consequences of compromise are many. First, compromise hardens your heart. It makes you deaf to God's convicting wisdom and blocks natural affection. Gradually, you experience less and less contrition, brokenness, and humility. You learn to live a hollow life of ritual with no true communion with God. Eventually, some become so hard that they can minister publicly without any guilt for their secret compromise.

That leads to another grave consequence. If you live in compromise as a minister, you will lead others into compromise. As a child, Samuel learned to live in compromise as if it were a normal way of life. He knew all the rituals of the altar, but he didn't know the Lord. In the same way, many churchgoers don't even *know* they are spiritually asleep. They've received a compromised lifestyle by osmosis from their spiritual leaders. So goes the pulpit, so goes the pew.

In its worst form, compromise can steal your soul. Many compromised churchgoers eventually take their eyes completely off of Jesus. They don't only leave their first love—they reject Christ completely. Therein, they reject the only sacrifice available for sin. Speaking of this danger, Hebrews 10:26-27 says:

> If we go on sinning willfully after receiving the knowledge of the truth, there no longer remains a sacrifice for sins, but a terrifying expectation of judgment and the fury of a fire which will consume the adversaries. (NASB)

If you reject the only sacrifice made for your sins, you will experience eternal separation from God after you die. Don't run after your selfish desires. It could cost your eternity!

Test Yourself for Symptom #5

How about you? Are you in compromise? Do you do anything against your conscience? Do you make "small surrenders" to the devil? Do you allow ungodly practices in your daily life? Do you condone ungodliness? Do you compromise in the media you consume—in movies, music, books, magazines? Do you compromise in how you relate to the opposite sex? In your speech? By neglect of the Bible, prayer, worship, evangelism, or fellowship?

Dear reader, if you are in compromise, you are almost surely spiritually asleep.

My Spiritual Diagnosis:

_____

_____

_____

_____

_____

_____

_____

SYMPTOM #6: A PERVERTED GOSPEL

The sixth symptom of spiritual sleepiness is *a perverted gospel.* I want to talk about an issue that I've witnessed often recently. Tragically, I see this issue more now than ever. Many preachers have abused and perverted the gospel of grace.

Now, true grace is a beautiful thing. Grace is both the intercession of Jesus and the divine assistance of the Holy Spirit in our lives. True grace saves us from the penalty of sin and also equips us to live a life of righteousness. As Paul said in Titus 2:11-12, "The grace of God has appeared, bringing salvation to all men, instructing us to deny ungodliness and worldly desires and to live sensibly, righteously and godly in the present age" (NASB). As Charles H. Spurgeon said, "Grace is the mother and nurse of holiness, and not the apologist of sin."[13] God's grace frees us to live close to Jesus.

But many preachers declare a different grace; a kind of "*sloppy agape.*" They say, "You do not need to obey Jesus' commands. Jesus fulfilled everything on the cross, so no requirements remain for you!" Others say, "All of your sins are forgiven—past, present, and future. The way you live could never change that!" This hybrid grace message is radically different than God's true grace.

False Grace vs. True Grace

You see, false grace says, "I can live in continual sin and still be right with God." True grace says, "Because I've been made right with God, I want to *live a life of righteousness.*"

False grace says, "I have grace, so I'm responsible for nothing." True grace says, "I'm responsible to cultivate intimacy with God so His grace can give me power over sin."

False grace says, "God loves me just as I am—so I'll stay this way." True grace says, "God loves me just as I am, but too much to leave me this way."

False grace says, "My sins are forgiven—past, present, and future—no matter what." True grace says, "My past sins have been forgiven, God is empowering me in the present, and God will forgive me as I confess my future sins."

In summary, false grace allows me to live a life of sin. True grace empowers me to live a life of righteousness.

I have watched the effect of this false grace message for decades. It causes waves of spiritual dullness and sleepiness to crash over churchgoers. Professing Christians learn to live in habitual sin without any conviction or call to repentance. Many abandon the fear of God and begin to live in sin under the banner of "freedom in Christ."

John Wesley saw the effects of hyper-grace preaching in his day. Some Methodists began preaching a gospel which Wesley described as "smooth and soft as cream, in which was neither depth nor stream . . . speaking much of the promises, little of the commands."[14] Wesley reported the dreadful results in the congregations that received this message:

> When I came to review the societies, with great expectation of finding a vast increase, I found most of them lessened by one-third; one entirely broken up. That of Newcastle itself was less by a hundred members than when I visited it before. And of those that remained, the far greater number in every place were cold, weary, heartless, dead. Such were the blessed effects of this gospel preaching! of this new method of preaching Christ![15]

I hope John Wesley's story challenges you to get the gospel right.

Test Yourself for Symptom #6

Preacher, do you pervert the gospel? Does your message cause your hearers to experience conviction of sin, or no? Do you keep the cross and repentance at the center of your message? Do you avoid subjects like sin, eternal hell, or separation from God? Does your message awaken your hearers to their need of salvation and repentance? Or does it give them a false sense of security while they continue in sin?

Churchgoer, do you pervert the gospel? Does your gospel allow you to live in continual sin without conviction? Do you feel offended when you hear preaching about the cross of Jesus Christ or repentance of sin? When was the last time your heart broke over your sins? Over the fate of the lost?

Friend, if you've perverted the gospel, there's no question. You are spiritually asleep.

My Spiritual Diagnosis:

_____

_____

_____

_____

_____

_____

_____

_____

SYMPTOM #7: A FALSE SENSE OF SECURITY DESPITE ALL THESE SYMPTOMS

The final symptom of spiritual sleep is a false sense of security. What is a false sense of security? To believe you are right with God when you're not. As we discussed, many professing Christians live in sin without conviction or repentance. Many are blinded by the false euphoria of entertainment and elaborate church meetings. Others are blinded by a false grace message. Others prayed a sinner's prayer but never received the new birth through true faith in Jesus Christ. They show most or all of the signs of spiritual sleepiness—fascination with entertainment, a selfish life-focus, compromise, neglect of prayer, a lack of burden for souls, and a perverted gospel. Yet they feel secure that God is pleased with them and will save them on the day of judgment. That is the ultimate danger a person can face.

Now, God wants us to experience *true security* through faith in Jesus. As Charles H. Spurgeon said, "It is not security, but carnal security, which we would kill; not confidence, but fleshly confidence, which we would overthrow; not peace, but false peace, which we would destroy."[16] God does not want His true children to doubt their salvation. But, as Jesus said, "You will know them by their fruits" (Matthew 7:16 NASB). True salvation always bears the fruit of repentance in the believer's life.

You see, God's will is not *security at any cost.* His will is that you become a new creation through faith in Jesus Christ; that you begin a *genuine* relationship with God, and find security *in your relationship with Him.* That is why He awakens us through conviction and leads us to repentance. If you will humble yourself before Him, confess your sins and ask Him to save you, He will transform you from the inside out. Many live far below that reality. They've never received freedom from sin, fear, and God's judgment, but they feel secure in a false idea of grace. Don't you want the real thing?

Test Yourself for Symptom #7

How about you? Are you secure in your salvation? If so, why? Is your security based on your good works, as if you could earn salvation? Is it based on your union with Jesus Christ, and His payment for your sins on the cross?

Should you have eternal security? Have you experienced the new birth—God's total renewal of your inner being through faith in Christ? Do you bear the fruit of salvation? Do you hunger for God? Do you hunger for prayer? Do you hate sin? Do you experience conviction when you sin? Have you *ever* experienced conviction of sin? Have you ever experienced profound godly sorrow that led you to true repentance—a total overhaul of your life?

My Spiritual Diagnosis:

_____

_____

_____

_____

_____

_____

_____

I'm convinced that many churchgoers have never been born again. They've gone through the motions but never been divinely apprehended by God's love. If you have a false sense of security, Jesus is calling you out of the darkness and into the light. You can have true security today if you repent of your sins and place your trust in Him.

AN ALARM FOR SLEEPING READERS

While reading this chapter, have you detected spiritual sleepiness in your life? Friend, I must warn you. *God* has awakened you to that reality. *The Holy Spirit* has convicted you of your sin. If you refuse His Word, He has no obligation to continue striving to bring you to Himself. If you refuse to humble yourself and surrender all to God, you will only fall asleep *more.* Your heart will harden, you will become spiritually dormant, and soon you may experience spiritual death—eternal separation from God in hell. I repeat—when you resist God's voice, you invite eternal death in the lake of fire.

YOUR SAMUEL AWAKENING

But there is hope for you. God loves you, and is still speaking to your heart right now. He longs to bring you into a true relationship with Himself. Just as God awakened Samuel out of sleep and revealed His true glory, the Lord wants to awaken you out of your spiritual dormancy and show you Jesus' true beauty. If you will let Him do that, He will totally reorient your passions, goals, worldview, and lifestyle.

But He will do more than purify your life. Just as God commissioned Samuel to carry His Word to sleepy Israel, God will *commission you* to carry His glory and eternal truth in your generation. Samuel, now is your time to wake up!

Are you hungry for true spiritual awakening? Turn with me to the next chapter, where we discuss God's Samuelite call for every spiritual sleeper.

CHAPTER THREE

Samuels Awakening

*And the Lord came and stood, calling as at other times,
"Samuel! Samuel!" And Samuel said, "Speak, for your servant
hears." Then the Lord said to Samuel, "Behold, I am about to
do a thing in Israel at which the two ears of everyone who hears
it will tingle.*

(1 Samuel 3:10-11 ESV)

Samuel lived in an age of tragic spiritual sleepiness; a generation "which knew not the Lord" (Judges 2:10 KJV). Both priest and people lived in spiritual darkness. High Priest Eli had lost most physical eyesight (1 Samuel 3:2)—but much more tragically, he had lost spiritual vision. As a result, the whole land fell under a deep spiritual fog. Samuel inherited this spiritual sleepiness from Eli.

But Samuel would not sleep forever. Soon, God would awake him in the middle of the night. Calling Samuel by name, God would sovereignly jar Samuel's heart, bringing him out of dead religion and compromise and into intimacy with the Father. No longer would he only know holy *things*. He would know the *Holy God!*

Through this awakening, God would set Samuel immediately into his prophetic calling. First, Samuel would bring the piercing word of the Lord to Eli, his own spiritual father. Then, he would carry God's accurate prophetic word to all Israel for his whole life:

> *And Samuel grew, and the Lord was with him and let*
> *none of his words fall to the ground. And all Israel from*
> *Dan to Beersheba knew that Samuel was established as a*
> *prophet of the Lord.* (1 Samuel 3:19-20 ESV)

Yes, awakened to God's eternal purposes, Samuel would never turn his back on the Lord. Instead, God would use him to begin a prophetic movement in Israel. The uncommon would become common again: God's Word, presence, and purposes would be known to the many.

A DIVINE WAKE-UP CALL

Are you spiritually asleep like Samuel was? Again, I'm not asking if you go to church, practice religion, know the latest worship songs, quote the Bible, tithe, or speak fluent

Christianese. You could do all these things and yet remain dead to God.

This is what I do mean: do you show signs of spiritual sleepiness? Are you fascinated with entertainment? Do you have a selfish life-focus? Do you compromise in any way? Do you lack a strong prayer life? Do you lack a burden for souls? Have you believed or preached a perverted, permissive gospel? Have you lived under a false sense of security? Friend, if you're spiritually asleep, God is letting forth a divine wake-up call!

GOD'S WILL FOR YOUR LIFE

It's not God's will for you to live in spiritual dormancy! Just as God awakened Samuel out of sleep, God longs to awaken you from your spiritual sleepiness, teach you His voice, set you into His calling, and ignite you for His purposes! You can experience the power, holiness, and glory of the living God.

Reader, are you hungry to experience a spiritual awakening like Samuel's? I want to show you four key elements of Samuel's awakening that God longs to activate in your life.

WAKE UP TO ETERNAL REALITIES

First, God wants to awaken you to eternal realities. Samuel lived in the presence of God and the holy objects of the temple. He knew the rhetoric, forms, and formalities of religion. But as a result of Eli's compromise, Samuel did not know the God of salvation. For this reason, I believe Samuel felt shocked when he first encountered the Lord. For years he'd heard from Eli *about* God—but now he'd heard *from God Himself!*

Like Samuel, millions of involved churchgoers have never had an authentic encounter with God. They live around holy things—they study in seminaries or Bible colleges, play in worship bands, sit in the pews, or even preach in pulpits—but they've never truly met the Lord of glory. A Samuelite awakening ushers such spiritual sleepers into *real* intimacy with Christ. God apprehends them with His eternal love; the religious churchgoer *truly meets the Lord* and experiences His glory, mercy, and holiness. This may hurt at first, but soon leads to exuberant joy!

This element of the Samuelite awakening transformed the Apostle Paul's life. After Paul truly encountered God, he lived overwhelmed by Christ's glory and secure in God's eternal love for him. Having encountered the living Savior, Paul cried,

> Who shall separate [me] from the love of Christ? . . . For I am sure that neither death nor life, nor angels nor rulers, nor things present nor things to come, nor powers, nor height nor depth, nor anything else in all creation, will be able to separate [me] from the love of God in Christ Jesus our Lord. (Rom. 8:35, 38-39 ESV)

The more Paul encountered the Lord, the more he understood that God had "bought [him] with [the] price" of Jesus' blood (1 Corinthians 6:20 ESV). Because of this, he didn't have to convince himself to follow Jesus day after day. Overwhelmed by the gracious person of Jesus, Paul could go nowhere but where He led. Late in life, Paul's cry remained the same—"that I may know [Christ] and the power of His resurrection and the fellowship of His sufferings, being conformed to His death" (Philippians 3:10 NASB). Like Samuel, Paul's fire never waned.

This element of the Samuel awakening revolutionized John Wesley's life, too. As a young man, Wesley had detailed theology and rigorous piety—yet, much like Samuel, he did not yet know the Lord. After years of rigorous religious effort, John Wesley had a genuine encounter with the living God when he least expected. Wesley described his experience:

> In the evening I went very unwillingly to a society in Aldersgate Street, where one was reading Luther's preface to the Epistle to the Romans. About a quarter before nine, while he was describing the change which God works in the heart through faith in Christ, I felt my heart strangely warmed. I felt I did trust in Christ, Christ alone, for salvation; and an assurance was given me that He had taken away my sins, even mine, and saved me from the law of sin and death.[17]

It was then that God began to radically transform Wesley's life. Soon, Wesley would begin leading thousands to Jesus—and continue faithful for his whole life!

I want to share a personal account that reflects this point. I once visited Leonard Ravenhill's library and office in his former home in Lindale, Texas. For years, Ravenhill spent long hours communing with God in that room, and God used his life powerfully for His glory. As I entered the room, I felt captivated by the sense of eternity I experienced. Soon, I spotted a wooden plaque that read: "Keep me eternity-conscious." Even Ravenhill wanted a daily reminder of God's call to keep eternity in view. We must not get distracted by the meager and temporal fascinations of this present world. As Paul commanded, we must "set [our] affection on things above, not on things on the earth" (Colossians 3:2 KJV).

Are you living in powerless religion? Are you around holy *things* but far from the *Holy God?* Today, God wants to divinely apprehend you with His love and awaken your heart to His eternal reality. Without this, you can never join a Samuel generation! Will you allow God to awaken you to His glory?

WAKE UP TO TRUE REPENTANCE & SURRENDER

Second, God wants to awaken you to His call to repentance and true surrender. When God awakened Samuel, He first tested his willingness to obey. Before anything else, God commanded Samuel to a horrifying task: he must declare judgment on his spiritual father Eli. 1 Samuel 3:15 reveals that "Samuel was afraid to tell the vision to Eli" (ESV). Samuel was Eli's mentee and protege—and a young boy protege at that. He loved and respected Eli. Can you imagine having to deliver such a word to your elder, mentor, and spiritual father? Yet he only had two options—surrender to God or continue in Eli's compromise. How could he live if he let the word simmer in his heart, unreleased? Having heard God's voice, Samuel found himself at a point of fearful embarkation; a moment in which God called him to step far out of his comfort zone and into surrender and true obedience. Samuel wondered how he would deliver the word, but knew he must—lest he disobey the God who spoke to him.

Samuel's awakening teaches a vital lesson: the only thing that qualifies you is that which purifies you. You cannot receive God's calling without first experiencing "the fear of the Lord [which] leads to life" (Proverbs 19:23 NASB).

This lesson manifests in the life of Isaiah. Long before the prophet Isaiah could say, "Here I am! Send me" (Isaiah 6:8 ESV), he had to cry, "Woe is me! For I am lost; for I am a man of unclean lips!" (Isaiah 6:5 ESV). Isaiah had lived a generally pure external life, and had already begun to speak for God. But before God could use Isaiah, He had to scorch his conscience and purify his heart. Soon, Isaiah would encounter God's holiness, leading to the shocking revelation of his own sinfulness.

As Bible teacher H.A. Ironside explained:

> Beholding God . . . [made Isaiah] realize his own unworthiness and the corruption of his own heart. Isaiah saw himself in the light of the Lord's infinite holiness. It is ever thus when man is brought consciously into the presence of God . . . When [Isaiah] saw himself in the light of the holiness of God, he at once acknowledged his own sinfulness; and moreover, he recognized the fact that he was surrounded by men, who, like himself, were of unclean lips.[18]

During this encounter, Isaiah would confess his sinfulness, and God would forgive him, saying: "Your iniquity is taken away and your sin is forgiven" (Isaiah 6:7 NASB). Only then did God call Isaiah, saying, "Whom shall I send, and who will go for Us?" (Isaiah 6:8 NASB). This led Isaiah to completely surrender to God's will, crying: "Here I am! Send me!" (Isaiah 6:8 ESV).

Hebrews 12:29 says, "God is a consuming fire" (NASB). If you would be used by God, you must first be heart-stricken by the fiery nature of God. It's impossible to see God in all His fullness, for God says, "No man can see Me and live!" (Exodus 33:20 NASB). Yet you must truly behold Him as He grants you.

When you encounter God's holiness, you will naturally respond with fear, shock, and awe. You will become keenly aware of how you've sinned against Him. Have you allowed perversion to dictate your life? Have you allowed lies, hypocrisy, jealousy, pride, envy, and arrogance to guide your way? God's holy presence will bring all things to light, leading you to holy brokenness. Seeing the depths of your own sin, you will cry, "God, how could I have been so blind? How could I have been so deaf? How have I been so asleep in such a tragic, ungodly hour?"

Such an encounter requires deep repentance. Yes, to truly walk in a Samuel anointing, you must die to your sin and lose yourself in God's purposes. You must be willing to turn from every pattern of compromise and sin and turn your face to Jesus. You must look straight in His face and fear to look to the right or the left. God will strengthen you to do this, but you must humble yourself and submit your will to God.

A Samuel awakening will not make you perfect in practice, but it will purify your motives. Yes, a true prophetic Samuel calling searches past the exterior life, deep into the motivations of the heart—what I call the *origin of actions.*

When God intends to raise up a Samuel, He first forces the believer to ask: "Why do I do what I do?" They feel they must review their lifestyle, relationships, thought life, ministry, preaching, and more. To ministers, God probes: "*Why do you minister? Do you minister for your own reputation? Do you use clever tricks to move people, or are you truly living as My mouthpiece?*" When passing through a Samuel awakening, many have discovered with great grief that they had lived for selfish purposes—selfishness, self-preservation, self-performance, self-fulfillment, selfish lusts, and more.

This aspect of the Samuel awakening first pierces the soul, but soon leads to a life of joyful surrender. To surrender is not merely to accept *your responsibility,* but to respond to *God's ability in your life.* God wants to awaken a heart of passion within you that will move you in perfect obedience to His will. He is ready to send His grace to lead, guide, and strengthen you in obedience. But will you surrender to His gracious influence?

Only through this fiery calling can you be qualified to carry His glory and kingdom. If you don't undergo this process, you'll prove dangerous to God's purposes—even if you're gifted and anointed. You may look effective in the eyes of the worldly church system. You may display signs, wonders, and miracles. You may even experience what you believe are 'lightning-bolt' experiences with God's glory. But if you don't *truly* yield your heart to God, your sin and compromise will trickle down to your flashy audiences—and even worse, to your spiritual sons and daughters. Worst of all, if you continue in this, then at the judgment, you'll hear Jesus say, "I never knew you; depart from me, you [worker] of lawlessness!" (Matthew 7:23 ESV).

Reader, if you would join a Samuel generation, you must experience the radical cleansing of God's holy visitation. Only then will you be qualified to carry His Word to a dying world!

WAKE UP TO THE GOSPEL OF JESUS CHRIST

Next, God wants to awaken you to the true gospel of Jesus Christ. Every man or woman who God has ever truly awakened has wonderfully encountered the glorious gospel—that "while we were still sinners, Christ died for us" (Romans 5:8 ESV).

We cannot know the Holy God personally and powerfully until we receive forgiveness of our sins. Ephesians 2:1-3 reveals our desperate spiritual state without Jesus:

> You were dead in your trespasses and sins, in which you formerly walked according to the course of this world, according to the prince of the power of the air, of the spirit that is now working in the sons of disobedience. Among them we too all formerly lived in the lusts of our flesh, indulging the desires of the flesh and of the mind, and were by nature children of wrath, even as the rest. (NASB)

Paul's conclusion is grave: without Christ, we're not merely bad, nor even "not good"—we are dead! The Greek word here translated "dead" is *nekrous*, which can mean "a dead body [or] a corpse."[19] Until we understand, believe, and respond to the gospel of Jesus Christ, we are spiritual corpses, unable to know God or live holy lives. Without Christ, we are cut off from communication with the Lord—dead to His voice, His touch, His power, His glory, and His presence, and headed for eternal death in hell.

Yes, "The wages of sin is death" (Romans 6:23 ESV). As D.L. Moody explains, we will suffer eternal death if we break even one of God's commandments:

> These ten commandments are not ten different laws; they are one law. If I am being held up in the air by a chain with ten links and I break one of them, down I come, just as surely as if I break the whole ten. If I am forbidden to go out of an enclosure, it makes no difference at what point I break through the fence. "Whosoever shall keep the whole law and yet offend in one point, he is guilty of all." "The golden chain of obedience is broken if one link is missing." [20]

What is the solution to our desperate problem of sin and spiritual death? The cross of Jesus. You see, God paid a high price to set you free from sin and spiritual sleepiness. Jesus the Son of God willingly laid His life down for you. On the cross, He bore the wrath of God you deserve so you wouldn't have to. Isaiah explained it this way in Isaiah 53:5-6:

> He was pierced through for our transgressions,
> He was crushed for our iniquities;
> The chastening for our well-being fell upon Him,
> And by His scourging we are healed.
> All of us like sheep have gone astray,
> Each of us has turned to his own way;
> But the Lord has caused the iniquity of us all
> To fall on Him. (NASB)

This is the horror and the beauty of the cross: Jesus hung bloodied and naked before all the world so you could stand innocent and forgiven before God. As Paul declares, "God made him who had no sin to be sin for us, so that in him we might become the righteousness of God" (2 Corinthians 5:21 NIV). Because of this great sacrifice, no sinner is too far from God's reach. If anyone believes in Jesus' sacrifice, turns from sin and sleepiness, and receives Christ as Master and Savior, God's supernatural grace will forgive their trespasses, set them free from sin, and awaken them to God's beauty.

No matter your spiritual condition, you desperately need the transformation and pardon of the cross of Jesus Christ. This great inner miracle only happens by God's grace. Ephesians 2:8-9 says: "By grace you have been saved through faith; and that not of yourselves, it is the gift of God; not as a result of works, so that no one may boast" (NASB). The Greek word here translated "grace" is *chariti* which means "a gift or blessing."[21] God forgives our sins and restores our lives as an undeserved gift, not as a deserved reward for our hard work.

Yes, as a gift, God unites us with Christ in His crucifixion and resurrection. As Paul says, "We were buried therefore with [Christ] by baptism into death, in order that, just as Christ was raised from the dead by the glory of the Father, we too *might walk in newness of life*" (Romans 6:4 ESV, emphasis mine). In light of this spiritual reality, Paul boldly proclaims: "If the Spirit of him who raised Jesus from the dead dwells in you, he who raised Christ Jesus from the dead will also give life to your mortal bodies through his Spirit who dwells in you" (Romans 8:11 ESV). Just as God awakened Samuel out of sleep, God wants to awaken you out of spiritual death through the gospel.

If you would join a Samuel generation, you must cry with Paul, "By the grace of God I am what I am" (1 Corinthians 15:10 NIV)! You must identify yourself only by God's grace, Jesus' cross, and the Spirit's power. Then God can cleanse your sins, awaken your heart to His purposes, and activate you in your calling! Hallelujah!

WAKE UP TO GOD'S CALLING

Next, God wants to awaken you to His calling. When God awakened Samuel, the prophet became consumed by God's call. God's calling became as a fiery combustion exploding in Samuel's heart. Samuel didn't have to "put on" the call—and he surely couldn't turn it off. It engulfed his entire being. He *became the message* as he became one with God Himself. As a result, he became God's mouthpiece to his generation.

God wants to awaken you to His calling much like He did with Samuel. This Samuelite call is not restricted to an elite group. God doesn't merely look to use the respected, the wealthy, or the talented. He doesn't look at the titles in front of your name or the degrees behind your name. He doesn't look at who you are, who your family is, or what denomination you belong to. God is looking for willingness—for men and women who will say: "Jesus, I give my life for the gospel. I will not compromise Your calling. I lay everything down, because I *must* know You, and I must make You known to my generation."

God is calling every obedient Christian to two important tasks. If you would join the Samuel generation, you must fulfill His Great Commission and live a prophetic lifestyle.

Calling #1: Fulfill God's Great Commission

First, God is calling you to fulfill the Great Commission. What is the Great Commission? Jesus tells us in Matthew 28:18-20:

> All authority in heaven and on earth has been given to me. Therefore go and make disciples of all nations, baptizing them in the name of the Father and of the Son and of the Holy Spirit, and teaching them to obey everything I have commanded you. (NIV)

Jesus calls us to make disciples of all nations. That means we must make Jesus known to others who will also make Jesus known; we must "preach the gospel to all creation" (Mark 16:15 NASB). What gospel must we preach? Paul tells us:

> For I delivered to you as of first importance what I also received, that Christ died for our sins according to the Scriptures, and that He was buried, and that He was raised on the third day according to the Scriptures.
> (1 Corinthians 15:3-4 ESV)

Jesus reiterates the gospel we must preach in Luke 24:47-48:

> Thus it is written, that the Christ should suffer and on the third day rise from the dead, and that repentance for the forgiveness of sins should be proclaimed in his name to all nations, beginning from Jerusalem. You are witnesses of these things. (ESV)

This Great Commission is God's mandate for the whole church. Many think that God only calls pastors or evangelists to preach the gospel. Others say, "The Great Commission was only for the biblical apostles." But no. God requires every Christian—including you—to obey the Great Commission. Whether you are a pastor, a janitor, a student, or an average joe with an average job, God has called you to win the lost to Jesus.

In every generation, Samuels bring God's kingdom to bear on society through this Great Commission. In fact, I believe God sent out every true missionary in history by a Samuelite awakening.

Here's what I mean. Samuel received a revelation of God which captured his heart, purified his life, and catapulted him into God's call. By this same experience, God catapulted Adoniram Judson, Amy Carmichael, C.T. Studd, Hudson Taylor, and many other faithful missionaries into the world's darkest lairs as lights in the darkness. God awakened these servants to the reality of His glory, and they *had to go.* They didn't see God's Great Commission as merely a noble Christian endeavor; God's call captured them, and it seemed *harder to stay* than to go. They saw people groups dying without Jesus, heading for an eternal hell. They considered no suffering too great if they could only save those perishing without Jesus.

This leads me to ask—are you willing to go for Jesus? One day, every living soul will either inhabit heaven or hell for all eternity. Those who die without Christ will have no hope for reprieve or forgiveness. They will suffer in the lake of fire, "where their worm does not die and the fire is not quenched" (Mark 9:48 ESV). You hold the gospel that can save them in your hands. Will you call the world to a decision? Will you bring the reality of Jesus into every sector of society? If not, you can't claim to live a Christian life. You can't separate the Great Commission from Christian living—they go together like a hand in a glove. As Charles H. Spurgeon said, "Have you no wish for others to be saved? Then you are not saved yourself. Be sure of that."[22]

But maybe you say, "God hasn't called me to evangelize!" I exhort you with the words of Salvation Army founder William Booth:

"Not called," did you say? Not heard the call, I think you should say. He has been calling loudly ever since He spoke your sins forgiven—if you are forgiven at all—entreating and beseeching you to be His ambassador. Put your ear down to the Bible, and hear Him bid you go and pull poor sinners out of the fire of sin. Put your ear down to the burdened, agonized heart of humanity, and listen to its pitying wail for help. Go and stand by the gates of Hell, and hear the damned entreat you to go to their father's house, and bid their brothers, and sisters, and servants, and masters not to come there. And then look the Christ in the face, whose mercy you profess to have got, and whose words you have promised to obey, and tell Him whether you will join us heart and soul and body and circumstances in this march to publish His mercy to all the world. 23

God's already called you to win the lost. Will you receive His call, or reject it?

Calling #2: Live a Prophetic Lifestyle

Second, God is calling you to live a prophetic lifestyle. God calls *everyone in the body of Christ to be prophetic.* In Acts 2:17-18, Peter declares an Old Testament prophecy to announce a New Testament reality:

And in the last days it shall be, God declares,

that I will pour out my Spirit on all flesh,

and your sons and your daughters shall prophesy,

and your young men shall see visions,

and your old men shall dream dreams;

even on my male servants and female servants

in those days I will pour out my Spirit, and they shall prophesy. (ESV, emphasis mine)

I want to clarify what this *really means*. Many have a spooky or mystical understanding of prophecy. They ask, "Does this mean we will all be like Old Testament prophets? Does this mean we should call ourselves 'prophet Bill' and 'prophet Susie'?" I want to simplify this for you.

Paul explains prophecy this way: "One who prophesies speaks to men for edification and exhortation and consolation" (1 Corinthians 14:3 NASB). Peter explains it this way: "Whoever speaks, is to do so as one who is speaking the utterances of God" (1 Peter 4:11 NASB). To be prophetic is to burn for what God burns for; to feel what God feels, think what God thinks and then say what God says. In seven short words—to know God and make Him known.

As Jewish scholar Abraham Joshua Heschel said, "The prophet's word is a scream in the night. While the world is at ease and asleep, the prophet feels the blast from heaven."[24] Prophetic Christians hear an octave higher than the popular religious world, for they tap into the very heart of God. They cannot amalgamate into the mediocrity of popular Christianity, nor can they settle for the asceticism of lifeless religion. They have met God Himself, and they must bring God's weighty presence to bear on their generation.

Prophetic people cannot bear spiritual compromise; they feel deeply grieved at things others never even notice. Their hearts break when they see ministries full of adultery, greed, doctrinal error, moral compromise, and spiritual sleepiness. Through holy grief, God grips them in private prayer and grips men through their public preaching. In this way, their lives and preaching bring substance to the dead religious world.

In the Old Testament, God said, "I will restore to you the years that the swarming locust has eaten" (Joel 2:25 ESV). Several verses later, God revealed one way He would fulfill this promise: "I will pour out my Spirit on all flesh; your sons and your daughters shall prophesy" (Joel 2:28 ESV). God uses prophetic people to repair and restore what dead religion has lost.

Prophetic Christians are either loved or hated. They so overturn comfortable Christianity and its false security that people either cry, "More, Lord!" or, "Get away from me, legalistic fanatic!" They act as God's divine interruption in history; as agents of awakening and revival in times of compromise and spiritual dearth. Yes, they must suffer the fires of reproach and persecution for their commitment to God; yet God uses them to spark spiritual fires of passionate, worshipful devotion in the church.

Christian, God wills for you to live a prophetic life. You can know God's voice, for Jesus said, "My sheep hear My voice, and I know them, and they follow Me" (John 10:27 NASB). You can know God's presence, for Jesus said, "If anyone loves me, he will keep my word, and my Father will love him, and we will come to him and make our home with him" (John 14:23 ESV). You can know God's Word, for Jesus prayed, "Sanctify them in the truth; Your word is truth" (John 17:17 NASB). And you can know God's power, for Jesus said, "You will receive power when the Holy Spirit has come upon you; and you shall be My witnesses" (Acts 1:8 NASB). Through these four influences, God wants to use you to make Himself known to your generation. He wants you to experience His voice, presence, Word, and power so you can reveal His goodness, holiness, and truth to a lost world and a compromised church. That's what it means to live a prophetic life. Will you receive the call?

WHEN GOD CALLS YOU BY NAME

Something supernatural happens when God calls you by name. After God called out "Samuel!" to the sleepy altar servant, Samuel's life was never the same again. He had heard the voice of God—and that voice he must follow! Oh, that you would experience the same *today*; that God would call you by name, touch you by His Spirit, and set eternity in your heart like wind in your sails. If you turn from sin, cling to the cross, and invite God to divinely stir your heart, He will impart a passion for His eternal purposes, and that passion will press for utterance at your lips. The words that come out will ignite the hungry and discomfort the compromised. Yes, God will use your life to spark spiritual wildfires among those He has placed in your life. You will be a Samuel in your generation!

God could call your name in many ways. Perhaps God is using *this very book* to call your name, wake you out of spiritual sleepiness, point you to the cross, and awaken you to His calling. Will you receive His call today? God doesn't want you to worship Him at a distance. He doesn't want your form, sacrifice, and religious show. He wants your heart. Dear Samuel, God is calling. Will you wake up?

CHAPTER FOUR

*The Spiritual DNA of
the Samuel Generation*

J ust as Samuel slept by the altar, thousands lay sound
asleep in churches worldwide. Just as God's voice awoke
Samuel from his sleep, God is now awakening a Samuel
generation—men and women who have encountered God's
glory, abandoned compromise, recovered the biblical gospel,
and joyfully received God's call. But what sets the Samuel
generation apart? What are some of its defining characteris-
tics? Let's open God's Word to understand the spiritual DNA
of the Samuel generation.

THE SAMUEL GENERATION: REVIVAL CATALYSTS

First, members of the Samuel generation are catalysts for revival. God used Samuel to carry restoration and reformation to sin-darkened Israel. In a time of spiritual declension, Samuel brought the presence of the Lord to bear on God's people. He didn't merely have good theology and ministry organization skills. No; he carried the people into an authentic encounter with God Himself. He restored the very hope and destiny of Israel—that God would receive glory through them.

1 Samuel 7 demonstrates this powerfully. God had returned the ark of the covenant to Israel, but Israel had not yet returned to the Lord. Standing before the idolatrous nation, Samuel lifted up a cry for repentance and restoration:

> If you return to the Lord with all your heart, remove the foreign gods and the Ashtaroth from among you and direct your hearts to the Lord and serve Him alone . . . He will deliver you from the hand of the Philistines. (1 Samuel 7:3 NASB)

What a bold message! And God sent powerful results in response to Samuel's fiery call to revival: "The sons of Israel removed the Baals and the Ashtaroth and served the Lord alone" (1 Samuel 7:4 NASB)! The people of Israel returned to the Lord in sincere repentance, and God responded by rescuing them from the enemy Philistine armies.

Revivalist Leonard Ravenhill said: "Revival is when God gets so sick and tired of people misrepresenting Him that He shows Himself." Friend, there comes a time in history when the Lord says, "I am tired of being misrepresented by this people. I want to restore my glory!" God begins to burn inside a generation, launching them out into His purposes. When that Samuel anointing begins to shake, man's fears flee, God's fire burns, and a sense of calling and destiny ignites within. God's people begin to cry, "Lord, I want to be Your voice, Your hands, Your feet! I don't want to live up and down, in and out—I want to be a walking move of God in my generation." God uses such men as torches to restore His glory in the land.

Samuel remained a fiery witness for God until he passed into eternal glory. Like Samuel, we must keep the prophetic fire burning all our lives. Deep into old age, we must remain *grey glorious gleaners;* elderly Holy Ghost radicals full of glory, gleaning souls, and carrying the kingdom of God with us. God has called us to no less. Till the day we pass into glory, may we be catalysts for revival.

THE SAMUEL GENERATION: UTTERLY AUTHENTIC

Second, the Samuel generation is utterly authentic. Samuel lived a life of authenticity. He reflected the Creator in his lifestyle, not only his words. Through Samuel's life, God prophesied: "I am still the God of Abraham, Isaac, and Jacob, and I am in your midst!" For this reason, Samuel wasn't everybody's favorite preacher. When he came near a village, they sent forward to ask, "Do you come in peace?" (1 Samuel 16:4 NIV). The people either loved or hated him because he was *real*.

In the same way, God has called you to bring something real into this generation. You are not merely called to impress people by "eloquence [and] human wisdom" (1 Corinthians 2:1 NIV). God has called you to proclaim the powerful gospel of the cross of Christ—not in word only, "but in demonstration of the Spirit and of power" (1 Corinthians 2:4 NASB). He has called you to carry the authentic presence of God into the dens of rebellion.

Many Christians *are* authentic—authentically angry at the unbelieving world. Whenever they preach, they seem to hoist spiritual machine guns and aim their raging bullets at the lost. May it never be so with us! Jesus never spoke with anger at the lost. As Charles H. Spurgeon said, "If we are to prevail with men, we must love them."[25] Amy Carmichael echoes, "A cup brimful of sweet water cannot spill even one drop of bitter water, however suddenly jolted."[26] If we want good success, our hearts must be filled to the brim with authentic love for the lost.

God used George Whitefield's authentic love for the lost to break the most hardened hearts. One of Whitefield's partners reported that he rarely preached without weeping for his listeners.[27] After one message, a listener told Whitefield, "I came to hear you with a pocket full of stones to break your head . . . but your sermon got the better of me, and broke my heart."[28]

You see, the world can smell a fake a mile away—but they can smell authenticity too. The Lord activates something in their hearts when they meet a Christian who beams with Jesus' glory. Their arguments fall to the ground when a word of knowledge reveals the secrets of their hearts or God heals them through the laying on of hands. When the glory of God touches eternity within a man (see Ecclesiastes 3:11), he realizes the true God has come near. His life is touched. He might not surrender to Jesus that day, but God embeds an eternal seed inside him that will haunt him until he either hardens his heart or bows before the King in repentance.

God delights to move in and through your life. But you must be authentic.

THE SAMUEL GENERATION: DEAD TO EGO, ALIVE TO GOD'S GLORY

Third, the Samuel generation has died to ego and come alive to God's glory. Samuel was concerned about God's glory, not his own. For this reason, Samuel walked in heavenly boldness.

Samuel showed his concern for God's glory in 1 Samuel 13. Israel had to face a terrifying Philistine army—"30,000 chariots and 6,000 horsemen, and [warriors] like the sand which is on the seashore in abundance" (1 Samuel 13:5 NASB). Israel's army cowered in fear, and many "hid in caves, in thickets, in cliffs, in cellars, and in pits" (1 Samuel 13:6 NASB). Seeing this terrible military danger, Saul, Israel's king, desired to offer a sacrifice to God to enter battle safely. However, he knew God's law didn't allow him to offer burnt and peace offerings. He waited for Samuel to come to Gilgal and offer a legal sacrifice to God—but after suffering seven days of overwhelming fear, Saul offered the burnt and peace offerings himself, contrary to God's law (1 Samuel 13:9). When Samuel learned of this, he didn't stay silent in fear of losing favor with the King (or even losing his life). Burning for God's glory, Samuel issued a fierce rebuke to King Saul:

> What have you done? . . . You have acted foolishly; you have not kept the commandment of the Lord your God, which He commanded you, for . . . the Lord would have established your kingdom over Israel forever. But now your kingdom shall not endure . . . because you have not kept what the Lord commanded you.
> (1 Samuel 13:11, 13-14 NASB)

God is jealous for His own glory. In Isaiah 42:8, He declares: "I am the Lord; that is my name! I will not yield my glory to another or my praise to idols" (NIV). God doesn't seek His glory out of divine egotism, but love for His people. As Jonathan Edwards said, "God in seeking his glory, seeks the good of his creatures; because the emanation of his glory . . . implies the . . . happiness of his creatures."[29] Only when God reveals His glory to our hearts do we experience ultimate joy, freedom, and victory.

God can seek His own glory, but you can't. Friend, if you seek your own glory, you will wallow in depression all your life. If you seek joy in your own greatness, you will never find it. But true joy will flow like a river when you ferociously seek God's glory above all else.

Many are trapped in man-centered ministry. They want to impress men, so they never truly surrender to God. Perhaps they begin with small compromises: they avoid sharing a prophetic word to guard their popularity or plans, or keep silent about the gospel to avoid the judgment of their loved ones. Friends, we must abandon these childish fears and find our identity in the fire of the Holy Ghost. As revivalist Samuel Chadwick said, "Let no man join us who is afraid, and we want none but those who are saved, sanctified, and aflame with the fire of the Holy Spirit."

Yes, too many Christians today live as worldly breakers instead of heavenly receptacles. In electricity, a breaker turns power on and off, whereas a receptacle receives power and carries it from one junction to another. God has called us to carry the fiery current of His power, glory, and purposes everywhere, and never turn off the switch.

God reserves the move of His Spirit for those that offer themselves as His receptacles. When we do, He may move in ways that surprise us. Not long ago, God poured out the joy of the Holy Spirit on a congregation while I preached a challenging message. It didn't seem logical, but brought powerful results. Many received freedom from years of bondage as God's fire swept through the room. I'd watched many of those people strive to walk in freedom for years with no success. We offered ourselves as receptacles, and God sent His holy power to ignite passion and freedom in those hungry hearts. He wants to do the same for you.

THE SAMUEL GENERATION REFUTES THE NAYSAYERS AND RESTORES THE COVENANT

Fourth, the Samuel generation defeats the world's doubt and restores confidence in God's covenant. Today, we constantly hear about "fake news." In Samuel's day, many cried that God's covenant was fake news: "We've heard all these stories about Mount Sinai and Moses—all of these superstitious ideas. That worked then, but we live in a new era." In the midst of this, Samuel came to refute the naysayers and turn away the fake news that God no longer cared for Israel. God destined Samuel to restore confidence in His covenantal promises by revealing His glory to Israel and the surrounding nations. God is jealous for His people to experience His covenant promises.

God promised Abraham: "In your seed [Jesus] all the nations of the earth shall be blessed, because you have obeyed My voice" (Genesis 22:18 NASB). God longs to fulfill this promise through a generation of fiery evangelists who will declare the beauty of Jesus to a dying world. In Jesus, God the Father has restored to us "dominion over . . . all the earth" (Genesis 1:26 ESV). We must therefore invade the whole earth with gospel preaching, believing that "every place where you set your foot will be yours" (Deuteronomy 11:24 NIV). Hallelujah!

God has called the Samuel generation to restore confidence in God's covenant promises so the nations may repent, receive God's freedom and joy, and glorify God forever. Your role is *monumental*. Will you dare to step out and fulfill it?

MILLENNIALS: YOU WILL BE A SAMUEL GENERATION

Many believe millennials will never reach this high Samuelite calling. Older generations fret about what havoc they will bring upon the United States. They cry, "These young folk are biblically illiterate!" You know what I say, millennials? You will become a Samuel generation.

The glory of God will fall upon you. God will wake you up. And when He does, you will step out in reckless abandonment to the purposes of Jesus. God will give life to something fresh through you since you will begin without the baggage and misconceptions of Eli's dead religion. You will not be sucked in by the spirit of this age, the lusts of the flesh, the lust of the eyes, and the pride of life. You will not let the spirit of religion bring death to you, because God will give you radical authenticity. Now is your time. Wake up from your sleep, and become all God has destined you to be.

CHAPTER FIVE

From Samuel to David

*The Lord said, "Rise and anoint him; this is the one." So Samuel
took the horn of oil and anointed him in the presence of his
brothers, and from that day on the Spirit of the Lord came
powerfully upon David.*
(1 Samuel 16:12-13 NIV)

The Lord is awakening a generation of Samuels. This
generation has woken up to God's voice, renounced
compromise, recovered the biblical gospel, received
God's call, and is growing in the prophetic. They have died to
ego, come alive to God's glory, and have become catalysts for
revival. When they speak, they defeat the world's doubt and
restore confidence in God's covenants. Yet their calling is not
singular; instead, they exist to activate the David generation.
Just as Samuel called and anointed David the worshiper-
king, the Samuel generation awakens fiery worshipers of
Jesus the King.

THE PROPHET ANOINTS THE WORSHIPER-KING

David lived as a lowly and faithful servant long before he reigned as a powerful king. A mere shepherd boy, he spent his days in the field tending to his father's sheep and worshiping the Lord. In those fields, he began to learn the secrets of intimacy with God which he would later sing in Psalm 23:1-3:

> The Lord is my shepherd,
> I shall not want.
> He makes me lie down in green pastures;
> He leads me beside quiet waters.
> He restores my soul;
> He guides me in the paths of righteousness
> For His name's sake. (ESV)

There in those fields, God conceived a kingdom and calling within David. David would grow to become a king, priest, and prophet. He would obtain uncanny access to God's glory and root himself in intimacy with God more than almost any Old Testament figure. He would fail God severely but return to God wholeheartedly. Therein, he would learn the secret pathways to God's heart: "You will not delight in sacrifice… [or] burnt offering…The sacrifices of God are a broken spirit; a broken and contrite heart, O God, you will not despise" (Psalm 51:16-17 ESV). But before David could experience any of these milestones, he had to be called out and anointed.

It was Samuel who God used to activate David in his calling. When Samuel came to Jesse's house, David was still in the field "tending the sheep" (1 Samuel 16:11 NIV). His own father refused to believe he could become king, but his Heavenly Father's heart was settled. When Samuel saw David, the Lord said: "Rise and anoint him; this is the one" (1 Samuel 16:12 NIV).

"So Samuel took the horn of oil and anointed him in the presence of his brothers, and from that day on the Spirit of the Lord came powerfully upon David." (1 Samuel 16:13 NIV)

MAY SAMUELS ANOINT DAVIDS!

Many modern-day Davids are just waiting to be called out and anointed.

The Samuel anointing always makes way for the Deliverer and King. Just as Samuel anointed David the worshiper-king, the Samuel generation awakens worshipers of Jesus the King. When God's people renounce compromise, believe the biblical gospel, receive God's call, and begin to flow in the prophetic, God pours out His glory and holiness among them, awakening worship deep in every heart. Prophets like Samuel spearhead authentic moves of God that activate worshipers in their ferocious pursuit of intimacy with God.

Having experienced God's power, Davids then long for God's heart. Their hearts learn what A.W. Tozer testified: "God is so vastly wonderful, so utterly and completely delightful that He can, without anything other than Himself, meet and overflow the deepest demands of our total nature, mysterious and deep as that nature is."[30] As a result, they burn intensely for Christ. As Tozer said, their "hearts . . . are 'fit to break' with love for the Godhead," for they "have been in the Presence and have looked with opened eye upon the majesty of Deity."[31]

IGNITED BY GOD'S EMOTIONS

Many seem shut out of this glorious experience because of *dead Deism*. Deism teaches that God has no active involvement in the world; He merely created us, wound up the clock, folded His arms, and has done nothing but watch since. What a deadly lie!

The Bible proclaims that God is both involved in and concerned for this world and everyone in it. He can be "grieved" (Ephesians 4:30)—especially through dead religion. He can "rejoice" (Zephaniah 3:17)—especially in passionate worship. David had profound encounters with these emotions of God. Moved by God's love, David declared, "As a father shows compassion to his children, so the Lord shows compassion to those who fear him. For he knows our frame; he remembers that we are dust" (Psalm 103:13-14 ESV).

David understood that God wanted a deep connection to his heart, and this sustained David as he pursued the call of God. In the same way, God's holy emotions alone can keep us burning for the call; as Paul says, "Christ's love compels us, because we are convinced that one died for all" (2 Cor. 5:14 NIV).

THE PURPOSE OF GOD'S MANIFEST PRESENCE

Yes, God loves to pour out love and compassion on His children. But He doesn't visit us merely to give us 'liver-shivers'. More importantly, God pours out His glorious presence to ignite worship, activate callings, and sustain obedience. God used Samuel's ministry to pour out His Spirit on David and awaken him to his calling; and God will use the Samuel generation to equip, activate, and accelerate others into their destinies and callings.

If the Holy Spirit lives in you, God has placed a calling on your life—and He wants you to stand up and walk in it. More than ever, I'm hungry to see the body of Christ obey God's call. I long for the day when the church unites to preach the gospel, cast out devils, heal the sick, raise the dead, and advance God's kingdom in the lairs of hell. Pastor Charles H. Spurgeon said, "If sinners be damned, at least let them leap to Hell over our dead bodies . . . let no one go unwarned or unprayed for." Oh, that we would share the same heart! As evangelist Reinhard Bonnke often says, let us spend our lives "plundering hell to populate Heaven!"

WAKING UP?

Has God begun to ignite a Samuel anointing in your heart? While reading this book, do you find yourself tired of religiosity? Do you feel your heart can no longer bear to go through the motions? Do you feel a burning inside to abandon compromise, seek God's face, preach God's Word, and demonstrate God's power so God's kingdom can advance in your generation? I tell you, God has activated something in you. You might have only meant to read a book, but God intended to give you an authentic experience with His glory that would change your life forever.

I remember the first time I felt that stirring within. Over thirty years ago, God radically touched my life, rescued me from drugs and perversion, and set a flame inside of me. Today, by God's grace, I am burning more than ever before. The Samuel anointing came upon me, ignited the Samuelite call within, and God has kept me burning to this day. Perhaps God is doing the same thing for you right now. If so, now is the time to consecrate your heart to God. Turn with me to the next chapter, where together we will make a Samuel commitment. I pray you'll never be the same.

CHAPTER SIX

My Samuel Commitment

I n this final chapter, I will explain the practical commitment you must make to experience a Samuel awakening. If you want to become an instrument of God's glory in the face of compromise, sin, dead religion, apathy, and false doctrine:

1. You must deeply repent of *all* sin and sleepiness.
2. You must commit to a life of radical, humble prayer.
3. You must embrace the true, biblical gospel.
4. You must receive God's call to fulfill the Great Commission and live a prophetic lifestyle.

CONDITION #1: YOU MUST DEEPLY REPENT OF ALL SIN AND SLEEPINESS

First, you must deeply repent of *all* sin and sleepiness. Proverbs 28:13 says, "Whoever conceals his transgressions will not prosper, but he who confesses and forsakes them will obtain mercy" (ESV). In Revelation 3:19, Jesus declares, "Those whom I love, I reprove and discipline, so be zealous and repent" (ESV). To experience a Samuel awakening, you must first honestly review your life before God. Perhaps you've hidden certain areas of your heart from loved ones. You must open even those areas to God's searchlight. Once exposed, the Holy Spirit will do His beautiful work: He will convict you of sin, lead you to repentance, and grant you glorious freedom before God.

If you want to experience true Christianity, you must embrace this divine truth: *while God does not condemn His children, He does convict them.* Conviction is a wonderful work of the Holy Spirit wherein God addresses sin and compromise in our lives. Many modern Christians and leaders have mistaken conviction for condemnation, and therefore have spurned God's convicting power. Sadly, many have even misinterpreted the Bible to comfort compromised believers in their sin. You don't have to make the same mistake.

Hebrews 12:1 says, "Let us also lay aside every weight, and sin which clings so closely, and let us run with endurance the race that is set before us" (ESV). This glorious verse does not call for condemnation or legalism. Instead, it graciously demands that you deal with sin in your life. God's grace will enable you—but first, you must do your part. You must submit your will to God and commit to seek deeper places in His holiness, power, and glory. When you faithfully do this, His grace will provide unending power to stay free from the clutches of sin and compromise! 1 Corinthians 10:13 will become your reality:

> No temptation has overtaken you that is not common to man. God is faithful, and he will not let you be tempted beyond your ability, but with the temptation he will also provide the way of escape, that you may be able to endure it. (ESV)

CONDITION #2: YOU MUST COMMIT YOURSELF TO RADICAL PRAYER AND HUMILITY

Second, to experience a Samuelite awakening, you must commit to a life of radical prayer. You cannot and will not experience the Samuelite awakening unless you fulfill this condition. You can't experience Samuel's anointing unless you continually experience Samuel's God.

Prayer is the only place where God can break you; therefore, it is the only place God can prepare and qualify you to become a Samuel in your generation. If you want to be used by God, He ever calls you to pray. Be aware: if you commit yourself to a life of prayer, God will humble you profoundly. You will experience a meekness only known by those who live to behold God's glory and holiness in ever-increasing measure.

Hebrews 11:6 declares, "Anyone who comes to [God] must believe that he exists and that he rewards those who earnestly seek him" (NIV). This amazing promise of reward is not for the nominal disciple or the part-time Christian. God only promises reward if you 'earnestly seek Him' in full surrender! He beckons you to shut out the many distractions that steal you from the prayer closet. Then, you can gaze upon His glory and witness how the world and its trinkets grow dim.

CONDITION #3: YOU MUST EMBRACE THE TRUE, BIBLICAL GOSPEL

Next, you must embrace the true, biblical gospel. Nazarene founder P.F. Bresee said, "We are debtors to every man to give him the gospel in the same measure which we have received it." You can only fulfill your responsibility to your generation by believing and accurately presenting the gospel of Jesus Christ.

Unfortunately, Satan has sown other gospels in every hour of church history—ours included. The enemy hates the gospel and fights aggressively to alter its truth. He even attacks it from within Christendom. Why? The devil knows that only *the true gospel* can save humanity from hell and reach the dying world with God's power and love. False gospels had even arisen within the church in Paul's day. The Apostle Paul warned the Corinthians:

> If someone comes and proclaims *another Jesus* than the one we proclaimed, or if you *receive a different spirit* from the one you received, or if you accept *a different gospel* from the one you accepted, you put up with it readily enough.
> (2 Corinthians 11:4 ESV, emphasis mine)

Here, Paul rebukes the Corinthians for tolerating a perverted gospel. Paul's rebuke speaks loudly to our age. Just as God rose up Timothy to correct error in Ephesus, God wants to raise up modern-day Samuels to proclaim the true gospel with godly boldness!

To experience a Samuel awakening, you must say with Paul: "I am not ashamed of the gospel, for it is the power of God for salvation to everyone who believes" (Romans 1:16 ESV). The following Bible chart condenses the biblical gospel into four facts:

The Biblical Gospel in Four Facts

Fact #1: *You Have* *Sinned*	• **"All have sinned** and fall short of the glory of God . . . " (Rom 3:23 NASB) • **"Sin is the transgression of the law."** 1 Jn 3:4 KJV
Fact #2: *God Must* *Judge Sin*	• **"The wages of sin is death . . . "** (Rom 6:23 NASB) • "But for the cowardly and unbelieving and abominable and murderers and immoral persons and sorcerers and idolaters and all liars, **their part will be in the lake that burns with fire and brimstone, which is the second death."** (Rev 21:8 NASB)
Fact #3: *Jesus Died* *and Rose* *to Pay for* *Sin*	• **Christ also died for sins once for all,** the just for the unjust, so that He might bring us to God . . . " (1 Pet 3:18 NASB) • **"He did it to demonstrate his righteousness at the present time,** so as to be just and the one who justifies those who have faith in Jesus." (Rom 3:26 NIV) • **"The free gift of God is eternal life in Christ Jesus our Lord."** (Rom 6:23 NASB)
Fact #4: *You Must* *Respond* *to Jesus*	• **The Holy Spirit convicts you of sin:** " . . . When He comes, He will convict the world concerning sin and righteousness and judgment . . . " (Jn 16:8 NASB) • **You must repent of sin—turn from ungodliness:** " . . . Repent and turn to God and demonstrate [your] repentance by [your] deeds." (Ac 26:20 NIV) • **You must believe in Christ alone for salvation:** "Jesus said . . . 'he who believes in Me will live even if he dies' . . ." (Jn 11:25 NASB). • **Upon faith and repentance, God will change you from within by the Spirit of God:** "If anyone is in Christ, he is a new creation. The old has passed away; behold, the new has come." (2 Cor 5:17 ESV)

Dear friend, is this the gospel you believe? Any teaching that denies these truths is a lie, and any teaching that denies Jesus as the only way to salvation is a *heresy*. This is the gospel you must embrace to live a life like Samuel's. Will you believe it, obey it, and declare it to the world?

CONDITION #4: YOU MUST RECEIVE GOD'S CALL

Finally, to experience a Samuel awakening, you must receive God's call to fulfill the Great Commission and live a prophetic lifestyle. In Matthew 28:19, Jesus commanded, "Go therefore and make disciples of all nations, baptizing them in the name of the Father and of the Son and of the Holy Spirit" (ESV). God has placed you on earth to disciple all nations! You may be a young reader, an adult, or elderly. Your age matters little. Samuel heard the call as a young person and heeded. What matters is your willingness to yield to God's calling and purpose for your life.

In the previous chapters, God opened your eyes to the sleepiness of the modern church—and maybe even yourself. He then invited you to experience a Samuel awakening. Now the ball is in your court. What will you do with God's invitation?

Everything boils down to this: will you make a Samuel commitment, or continue living how you want? Will you listen to God's heart breaking over a church in sin and a world in utter darkness? Will you let His broken heart move you to reach the lost and call the church to repentance? Most people you encounter have no idea that they are lost and headed for eternal destruction! What will you do to make a difference for Jesus in your brief stay on earth?

WHAT IF?

I have often told my Bible college students that I don't want to die asking "What if?" "What if I had remained faithful to prayer and the Word of God?" "What if I had responded to the Great Commission and reached the dying world with the gospel?" "What if I had followed Samuel's example and listened when God called my name? What if I had then embraced a prophetic lifestyle?" "What if I had refused to allow passing distractions to hinder my passion for Jesus?" "What if I had chosen to pick up my cross and follow Jesus completely—by life or by death?"

James reminds us, "You do not know what tomorrow will bring. What is your life? For you are a mist that appears for a little time and then vanishes" (James 4:14 ESV). Dear reader, you have one life to live—and no rewinds. Maybe you will live 20, 40, or even 100 years. What is that compared to eternity? I implore you to listen as God calls your name! He invites you to His incredible eternal plan. He invites you to embrace a lifestyle of prophetic purpose. He would delight to share His power and glory with you. However, He will not force you into obedience. The choice is yours. The Lord Jesus awaits your response!

If you would like to make a Samuel commitment, I invite you to get on your knees and heartily pray the following format prayer. Perhaps you will want to pray it daily to renew your commitment to God and remind yourself of His calling on your life. Be sure to pray this from the depths of your soul and to add your own heart cry to these words.

My Samuel Commitment:
a Surrender Prayer

Dear God,
I want to carry Your glory in my generation.
I repent of all sin and refuse all compromise.
I cling to the only true gospel:
that Jesus Christ died on the cross
to pay for my sins, reconcile me to God,
and set me on fire for God's glory.
Seeking Your will alone, I turn from all apathy
and receive Your heavenly call.
From this day on, I will pray without ceasing,
preach without compromising,
listen to Your voice,
and obey without questioning.
I commit to live as Samuel did:
to be an agent of revival in the lives of my peers;
to reflect You in my lifestyle, not only my words;
and to live for Your glory alone—not my own.
I pray that through my life, You may defeat the world's doubt and
restore hope in Jesus' love.
In bold faith, I ask that You would awaken
me to Your glory more every day.
May Your kingdom come, and Your will be done
in my life as it is in heaven.
In Jesus' name, Amen.

IMPORTANT AFTERWORD

*Walking Out Your
Samuel Commitment*

E very generation reveals souls that refuse to settle for less than God's best. They seem to live in a realm beyond typical church experience—totally dedicated to Jesus, fueled by divine love, and continually crying for more of God. I have watched God arrest many hearts in this way through the years. It's as if God flips a divine switch inside them—He overwhelms them with His love, glory, holiness, and eternal purposes, and they are never the same again.

But the truth is that few can handle such fiery Christians. Most consider their expression of Christianity too fanatical—even dogmatic. Sleepy churchgoers feel uncomfortable in their presence (a telltale sign of conviction). As a result, many encourage them to calm down and blend in with everyone else. But how could they *slow down* after encountering Jesus in His glory? Unwilling to surrender to the lukewarm church, these red-hot saints inevitably suffer rejection from the religious culture around them. Like Samuel, they carry God's weighty glory, and their lives rebuke the culture's dead religion. In response, religion shows its fangs.

If you live Samuel's life, you will experience Samuel's persecution. Everyone loves a prophet after they die—but while they live, no one wants them. I believe many Christian churches would not even receive Jesus if He returned to earth and preached with the fire we see in Matthew, Mark, Luke, and John. With this considered, I want to share some important principles to help you follow through with your Samuel commitment. If you do not mature in these areas, you will struggle to stay faithful to God's prophetic calling.

PRINCIPLE #1. ADVANCE NO MATTER YOUR TRIALS, TROUBLES, OR TEMPTATIONS

First, you must seek to advance in your walk with God no matter what trials, troubles, or temptations surround you. God has adopted you in love and mercy, and invites you into glorious fellowship with Him in every season of life. Nothing could be more wonderful! As Paul says, God has "made [you] alive together with Christ" (Ephesians 2:5 ESV). Now 'made alive', you can live an abundant life of joy unspeakable and full of glory no matter your circumstances. You must cling to this reality. This new life you've received equips you to experience eternal joy and ongoing victory even while you encounter continual battles and trials.

You must always remember Paul's words: "Do not be conformed to this world, but be transformed by the renewal of your mind, that by testing you may discern what is the will of God, what is good and acceptable and perfect" (Romans 12:2 ESV). Even the strongest followers of Jesus live in a fallen world laden with sin and entrapments. Your enemy seeks with vehemence to destroy you. Do not conform.

What does this mean for you? You must commit yourself to God's Word and cling to what it says about your identity as God's child. You must not allow the temptations that surround you to pull you away from your Samuel commitment. You will be tempted. The enemy of your soul will seek to destroy you just as he sought to destroy Samuel and every other saint of history. The secret to success is to continually renew your mind. Let God's eternal truth penetrate the depths of your spirit—the devil cannot trump God's holy Word!

PRINCIPLE #2. DEVELOP AND GROW A VIBRANT AND SUPERNATURAL FAITH

Next, you must develop a supernatural faith in God and continually seek to grow that faith. Hebrews 11:1 says, "Faith is the substance of things hoped for, the evidence of things not seen" (KJV). The Greek word here translated "faith" is *pistis,* which means "trust [and] confidence."[32] To persevere in a Samuelite calling, you must grow confidence and trust in God; you must let faith come alive in you. Hebrews 11:1 reveals two dynamics of faith.

First, faith establishes a guarantee in your life; it is "the evidence of things not seen" (Hebrews 11:1 KJV). You can put stock in faith because it comes from God Himself. Faith assures you that your hope and calling in God are not passing pipe dreams; they have "substance" and reality. Faith provides a grounding you may earnestly cling to in times of difficulty. That grounding also directs you toward the future. It gives you courage and strength to move forward into the unknown, knowing that Jesus is "the captain of [your] salvation" (Hebrews 2:10 KJV)!

Second, faith supernaturally propels you into God's deeper purposes for your life. However, you can only grow in faith if you obey God's teaching about it. Faith develops in stages. If you remain teachable and humble, God will teach you deeper levels of faith in each season of your life.

You must develop faith by obeying God's call. You will experience God's glory only in proportion to your faith in and obedience to God's Word. It's not enough to experience a deep calling as Samuel—you must activate faith by surrender and obedience no matter what it costs or where it leads you.

PRINCIPLE #3. PERSEVERE NO MATTER THE COST

Next, you must learn to persevere in your prophetic calling no matter what it costs. Hebrews 12:1 says, "Since we are surrounded by so great a cloud of witnesses, let us also lay aside every weight, and sin which clings so closely, and let us run with endurance the race that is set before us" (ESV). James says, "Blessed is the man who remains steadfast under trial, for when he has stood the test he will receive the crown of life, which God has promised to those who love him" (James 1:12 ESV).

To become a Samuel in your generation, you must steadfastly persevere in God's call. I want to be honest—the masses will not line up to answer this Samuelite call. The Samuel call is not an invitation to celebrity Christianity, fortune, or fame. In truth, the price proves too high to pay for many. They cannot bear the shame of the cross, for they've embraced the tolerance of the age and redefined compromise as love. Many in the modern church live drunk on worldliness—and they will mock God's true call as antiquated legalism. In a generation fixated on the god of self, who will pay the price and lay their lives down so God can glorify Himself? Only some—even in this pressing hour.

I often say: "Salvation is a free gift you could never earn. But, the glory of God upon your life will cost you '*you*'!" In other words, Jesus paid the ultimate price through His death on a cross to ransom you from sin, and you could never add to His finished work. But, to know God's glory and prophetic calling, you must obey Jesus' call: "If anyone would come after me, let him deny himself and take up his cross daily and follow me" (Luke 9:23 ESV).

Jesus calls you to persevere and radically obey Him. He doesn't merely call you to soak in His presence—as glorious as that is. He calls you to be willing to receive rejection and hatred if necessary so your generation can witness God's authentic glory! Samuel restored the Word of God to Israel during his lifetime. Will you answer God's call to reveal His glory and purposes in your generation, and persevere no matter what it costs you?

PRINCIPLE #4. DEVELOP HOLY BOLDNESS IN THE FACE OF OPPOSITION

Finally, to persevere in your Samuel commitment, you must develop holy boldness in the face of opposition. The Apostle Paul said, "We are troubled on every side, yet not distressed; we are perplexed, but not in despair; persecuted but not forsaken; cast down, but not destroyed" (2 Corinthians

4:8-9 KJV). The first-century church experienced ongoing spiritual warfare as they advanced God's kingdom. The kingdoms of light and darkness clashed as fiercely as today, but Paul never wavered or flinched in the face of evil. He remained steadfastly bold, with a boldness firmly rooted in who he was in God and who God was in him! A realm of spiritual battle also rages in your life as a follower of Jesus. You must recognize this, or you will likely settle for a life of timidity and defeat. You must embrace Paul's call to remain bold in the spiritual battle.

Sadly, many never fulfill God's destiny upon their lives because they never allow the Holy Spirit to empower them with holy boldness. One of the main reasons God poured out His Spirit in the upper room was to empower the church with boldness. Though God has offered that boldness to all believers, many never experience it.

You will need more than strong character and a stubborn will to remain bold in your calling. You will need a continual supply of holy boldness. You must seek the Lord for a baptism in His power, and then for a continuing flow of His glory and fire. This alone will lead to the boldness you need. God wants you to experience Him in ever-increasing measures! He desires for you to experience fresh baptisms of His glory, fire, and power! His presence awaits your pursuit. Samuels, arise!

ABOUT KEITH COLLINS

Keith Collins has actively ministered for over 30 years. Keith's experience is vast, including missionary evangelism, church planting, international and domestic traveling ministry, college professorship, pastoring, and more. Keith is actively involved in itinerate ministry and speaks nationally and internationally on a regular basis. In recent years he served as the president of *The Brownsville Revival School of Ministry* and as the director of *FIRE School of Ministry*, which were both born out of the Brownsville Revival in Pensacola, FL. He currently lives in Charlotte, NC with his family including his wife Darla, three daughters, son in laws, and five grandchildren.

If you enjoyed *Samuels Arising*, please consider leaving a review for the book on Amazon. To learn more about Keith Collins and Generation Impact Ministries or to share any testimonies about *Samuels Arising*, please visit:

www.GenerationImpactMinistries.com
www.Facebook.com/KeithCollinsGIM

ACKNOWLEDGMENTS

I want to express my heartfelt thanks to JJ Weller, who played a big role in creating *Samuels Arising*. His editing skills helped me express the burden God laid on my heart. His excellence and abilities were invaluable to me. I strongly recommend him for any editing or writing project you need assistance with. To contact JJ, visit JJWellerMedia.com.

I want to share my gratitude and deep love to all the students and graduates I've been blessed to know over the last several years. To alumni of The Brownsville Revival School of Ministry, FIRE School of Ministry, and The Brownsville Ministry Training Center—you've blessed me! Our times in my classes and mentoring groups, in our home, on ministry trips, and more have been some of the great highlights of my life. You are etched upon my heart forever! May the eternal purposes of Jesus continue to lead you on your journey.

Most importantly, I want to say that I owe so much to my amazing wife and life partner Darla Collins! I can't imagine life or ministry without you, Darla! Your support, love, faith in Jesus, commitment to our family, and love for the body of Christ bless and strengthen me beyond description. I love you and look forward to many more years together!

NOTES

1 "Ligonier Ministries' State of Theology 2018." The State of Theology. 2018. Accessed June 06, 2019. https://thestateoftheology.com/.

2 Covenant Eyes, Porn Stats: *250 Facts, Quotes, and Statistics about Pornography Use (2018 Edition)*. Owosso, MI: Covenant Eyes, 2018. PDF, 23.

3 Ravenhill, Leonard. *Why Revival Tarries*. Baker Publishing Group, 2004. 31.

4 Barna Group. "New Marriage and Divorce Statistics Released." Barna Group. March 31, 2008. Accessed May 18, 2019. https://www.barna.com/research/new-marriage-and-divorce-statistics-released/.

5 Covenant Eyes, Porn Stats, 22.

6 Barna Group. "Porn in the Digital Age: New Research Reveals Ten Trends." https://www.barna.com/research/porn-in-the-digital-age-new-research-reveals-10-trends/. April 6, 2016. Accessed May 18, 2019. https://www.barna.com.

7 Hill, Stephen. *White Cane Religion; and Other Messages from the Brownsville Revival*. Shippensburg, Penn.: Destiny Image, 1997. 137.

8 "Lectures on Revivals of Religion: How to Promote a Revival by Charles Finney." Works of Charles G. Finney. Accessed May 18, 2019. https://www.gospel-truth.net/1835Lect_on_Rev_of_Rel/35revlec03.htm.

9 Bunyan, John. *Works of John Bunyan - Complete*. Kindle. Loc. 5388.

10 Grubb, Norman. *C.T. Studd: Cricketer & Pioneer*. 2014 ed. Fort Washington, PA: CLC Publications, 2014. Kindle Edition. 143. Capitalization Updated.

11 Smith, Oswald J. *The Revival We Need*. Shoals, Indiana: Kingsley Press, 2012. Kindle. Loc. 253.

12 Wesley, John. *Complete Bible Commentary: (Fully Formatted For E-Readers)*. Hargreaves Publishing. Kindle. Loc. 87305.

13 Spurgeon, Charles. *Morning and Evening—Classic KJV Edition*. Peabody, MA: Hendrickson, 2010. Kindle. Loc. 796.

14 Wesley, John. "Letter on Preaching Christ." Independent Methodist Arminian Resource Center. Accessed June 06, 2019. http://www.imarc.cc/one_meth/vol-02-no-10.html. Capitalization corrected.

15 Ibid.

16 Spurgeon, Charles. *Morning and Evening—Classic KJV Edition*. Kindle. Loc. 11139.

17 Wesley, John. *The Journal of John Wesley - Enhanced Version*. Christian Classics Ethereal Library. Kindle. Loc. 990.

18 Ironside, H.A., Litt.D. *Expository Notes on the Prophet Isaiah (Ironside Commentary Series Book 9)*. Neptune, NJ: Loizeaux Brothers, 1952. Kindle. Loc. 658.

19 "Ephesians 2:1 Strong's Lexicon." Ephesians 2:1 Parallel: And You Hath He Quickened, Who Were Dead in Trespasses and Sins;. Accessed June 06, 2019. https://biblehub.com/parallel/ephesians/2-1.htm.

20 Moody, D.L. *The Works of D. L. Moody, 25-in-1 [Illustrated], Overcoming Life, Secret Power, Men of the Bible, The Way to God, Heaven, Prevailing Prayer, Sowing and Reaping, Weighed and Wanting, Sermons*. Classic Christian Ebooks. Kindle. Loc. 16949.

21 "Greek Lexicon: Charis." Strong's Greek: 5485. χάρις (charis) -- Grace, Kindness. Accessed June 06, 2019. https://biblehub.com/greek/5485.htm.

22 Spurgeon, Charles H. *"SHE WAS NOT HID—NO. 2019—A SERMON DELIVERED ON LORD'S DAY MORNING, APRIL 15, 1888, BY C. H. SPURGEON, AT THE METROPOLITAN TABERNACLE, NEWINGTON."* Accessed June 5, 2019. http://www.spurgeongems.org/vols34-36/chs2019.pdf.

23 Booth, William. *THE LIFE AND WORKS OF GENERAL WILLIAM BOOTH and CATHERINE BOOTH of the SALVATION ARMY (Illustrated): 25 Works by the Founders of the Salvation Army with over 40 Illustrations.* Classic Christian Ebooks. Kindle. Loc. 15673.

24 Heschel, Abraham Joshua. "Selected Writings by Abraham Joshua Heschel." Institute for Jewish Ideas and Ideals. Accessed June 06, 2019. https://www.-jewishideas.org/article/selected-writings-abraham-joshua-heschel.

25 Spurgeon, Charles H. *The Soul Winner.* Louisville, KY: GLH Publishing, 2015. Kindle. Loc. 1842.

26 Carmichael, Amy. *If.* Fort Washington, PA: CLC Publications, 2011. Loc. 638.

27 Pratney, Winkie. *Revival: Principles to Change the World.* Pensacola, FL: Christian Life Books, 2002. Page 86.

28 Ibid.

29 Edwards, Jonathan. *The Complete Works of Jonathan Edwards: 59 Books with Table of Contents.* Kindle. Loc. 2853

30 Tozer, A.W. *The Pursuit of God.* Harrisburg, PA: Christian Publications, Inc., 1948. Kindle. Loc. 379.

31 Ibid. Loc. 377.

32 "Greek Lexicon: Pistis." Strong's Greek: 4102. πίστις (pistis) -- Faith, Faithfulness. Accessed June 08, 2019. https://biblehub.com/greek/4102.htm.